The Star Book for Ministers

Edward T. Hiscox

Second Revised Edition

Judson Press ® Valley Forge

Second Revised Edition
Copyright © 1994
Judson Press
Valley Forge, PA 19482-0851

Hiscox, Edward Thurston, 1814-1901.
The star book for ministers/ Edward T. Hiscox.—2nd rev. ed.
p. cm.
    Rev. by Frank T. Hoadley.
    ISBN 0-8170-0167-0
1. Pastoral theology—Handbooks, manuals, etc. 2. Bible—Quotations. I. Hoadley, Frank T. II. Title.
    BV4016.H5 1995
    253-dc20   94-38531

Printed in the U.S.A
15 14 13 12 11 10 09 08 07 06 05 04 03 02 01
10 9 8 7 6 5 4

Preface to Revised Edition

The Star Book for Ministers has been a trusted companion and reference for many generations of evangelical pastors, and as such it may accurately be described by the term *classic*, for it has stood the test of time as true classics do. One might logically ask, therefore, why there should be any need to revise it.

The answer to this question is found in the many changes that have come in the work of the church and of the minister during the past century. Observe, for instance, some of the differences between the author's day and ours:

In Hiscox's Day:

Weddings were frequently held in the bride's home.

Funerals were commonly held in the homes of the deceased persons.

The seriously ill were usually cared for in their own homes.

Pew rents were the usual method of financing

most of the work of the church.

The Sunday school was the only educational activity of the church.

Church property was commonly owned not by the church itself but by a "society."

In Our Day:

Weddings are usually held in the church building.

Funeral homes are the more usual locations for funerals, except those held in the church building itself.

The seriously ill are more commonly cared for in hospitals.

Pew renting is obsolete; stewardship, expressed through pledging and/or freewill offerings, is preferred.

Vacation school, Sunday evening groups, and many other educational programs have been added.

The church customarily holds title to the property in its own corporate name.

In preparing the present edition, it has been the object of the editors to make allowance for differences such as these, while still retaining as much of the original material as possible. Dr. Hiscox's language, not always easy to understand today, has been simplified to some extent in the interest of clarity. On the other hand, his suggestions for Scripture passages, the conduct of weddings and funerals, and other practical and spiritual matters of great importance to the church have been left intact.

The entire process of preparing the present edition has been carried out under authorization of the Hiscox family and in such a manner as we trust the author would approve if he were living.

The Editors

Preface to Second Revised Edition

Several generations have passed since Dr. Hiscox prepared the initial edition of his *Star Book for Ministers*, and more than a quarter of a century has elapsed since I was privileged to work on the 1968 revision of this classic handbook for pastors.

Over these years cultural changes such as those noted in our earlier preface have accelerated, affecting the ways in which churches perform their ministries. The message of Christ remains the same, but methods of interpreting and expressing it are affected by changing trends in society, even in the language we use to convey that message.

So the need for a second revision has arisen, and again I am grateful for being permitted to have a part in it. You will find that Dr. Hiscox's copious "Suggestions to Ministers" have been reorganized into six chapters, giving an overview of the pastor's work in our day, including some helpful suggestions. The large section of "Selections from Sacred Scripture" has been reorganized to make it easier to find materials you need. Many texts have been added, and a few omitted that are less useful in today's world. Information on parliamentary procedures has been simplified to make it more useful for churches.

The spirit and much of the content of the author's original work continue to be appropriate as we come to the twenty-first century, and so I have tried to maintain that. All Scripture quotations are in the King James Version, but their source is identified so that you can conveniently substitute one of the modern translations if you wish.

Dr. Hiscox was a Baptist, and he prepared the *Star Book* primarily for Baptist pastors. In spite of this focus, however, the book has long been well received by clergy of many denominations, and in this revision I have tried to retain its broad Christian appeal. Those of us who have been involved in this revision trust that Dr. Hiscox would have been pleased with it and that you will find this newest *Star Book* useful in your ministry.

Frank T. Hoadley
Gaithersburg, Maryland
June 1994

Contents

I

On Being a Pastor

I

On Being a Pastor

1. Entering the Christian Ministry

The very fact that you are holding this book in your hands indicates that you are probably the pastor (or one of the pastors) of a church, or that you are considering entering the Christian ministry. Or, just possibly, you may be a lay officer of the church, whose responsibilities make it important for you to understand and support the pastor's work. So let us begin the section "On Being a Pastor" with a chapter on what it means to be a minister of Jesus Christ. As we continue, we shall deal in other chapters with aspects of the ministry that are unique to the pastorate of a church.

Called to Minister

Most Christians believe in the idea of Christian vocation. By this they mean that the literal translation of the word *vocation*, which means "calling," is appropriate to whatever work we do. We believe that God calls us to use the talents given us in some way that will glorify God and contribute to the betterment of the world in which we live. We may be called by God to teach school, to care for the sick, to manufacture useful products, to prepare food, to care for children, to perform scientific research, or to provide wholesome entertainment. The list goes on. If we cannot in some way see God's calling in the work we do, we may want to reconsider our vocation.

The Christian ministry is a special type of calling. For some it may come in a sudden and dramatic fashion, such as God's call to Samuel in the night or Paul's shattering experience on the road to Damascus. For others it may be a slowly growing realization that professional ministry, above all other callings, is what they are best qualified to do. And for still others it may be the result of intense questioning and self-searching: "How can I best serve God in making this a better world?"

So important is our response that we need to test ourselves. If you sense a call of God to the ministry, there are questions you may ask yourself, such as: Is my commitment to Christ strong enough to withstand discouragement and disappointment? Do I care enough about other people that I can lay aside my own concerns, when necessary, in order to deal with theirs? Do I have sufficient education, or educational plans, to carry out my duties in a manner that will be pleasing to the Lord? Am I physically able to work long hours when necessary? Can I make myself clearly understood when I speak? It also helps to get the opinions of experienced ministers, such as active or retired pastors, who can counsel you. Some persons test themselves by enrolling in a theological school for a semester or two and accepting a small student pastorate or assistant pastorate under field work supervision so as to see what their new life would be like.

If you come through such testing and questioning firmly convinced that God wants you in the pastoral ministry, more power to you. If not, it is better that you know the truth and seek your calling in some other field where your talents can be better used.

Ordination

The process by which one becomes a Christian minister is called ordination. It is often preceded by a step known as licensing. Both licensing and ordination are actions of a specific local church of which the candidate is a member. The license to preach, as it is usually called, is an affirmation that the church believes the individual has the abilities, emotional stability, and spiritual sensibilities necessary for some form of gospel ministry and that this person is participating in systematic study to become fully qualified. Often the licensee is placed under the watchcare of an experienced pastor. Licensing is not the same as ordination; it is a step toward that event, usually preceding it by at least six months. A licensed pastor must be careful not to exceed the authority that the status confers. In many states or municipalities, for instance, a licensed preacher may not have the right to perform marriages.

The ordination process varies in different church bodies. In many or most denominations the candidate for ordination is expected to meet educational requirements that include four years of college and three years of seminary study, with the completion of appropriate academic degrees, and to have definite plans for a career of parish, missionary, or specialized ministry. Usually there is a department of ministry in the state, regional, or associational body to which the church belongs, and this body reviews the candidate in a general way to ascertain whether the candidate has qualifications for ministry. If so, the department will recommend to the local church that it call an ordination council—but not make plans for an ordination service until the council has acted.

In some associations there is a permanent ordination council that a church can call upon to advise it on the qualifications of a candidate; in others, a council is assembled at the church's invitation, often consisting of one clergy and one or two lay persons from each church in the association that responds to the call. Customarily the candidate has prepared a paper and reads it to the council, giving a bit of personal background, including the call to ministry, and the candidate's own understanding of Christian doctrine. The council then questions the candidate to understand more clearly what has been said (or perhaps left unsaid). In the questioning it is important to bear in mind that many traditions allow for a considerable degree of freedom in interpreting biblical and theological matters. The questioning is not for the purpose of determining whether the candidate's views coincide with those of individual council members but rather that they represent serious study and reflection and are held in good conscience. Would they be generally compatible with the teachings of most churches to which the candidate might be called as pastor?

Following the questioning, the candidate is then excused while the council deliberates and votes either that ordination should proceed or that it should be deferred until some future date (stating the reasons) or that the ordination should not take place.

Assuming that the council votes favorably, the church then feels free to proceed with the actual ordination service, to which it will invite guests from other churches of the association and from the community. There is plenty of room for creativity in the ordination service, but four ingredients in particular are customary: an ordination sermon, preached by an experienced pastor or a seminary professor; a charge to the candidate, outlining briefly what is expected of a pastor; a charge to the church, informing the congregation as to how they may effectively support the new ordinand's ministry; and an ordination prayer, during which all ordained persons present are invited to place their hands symbolically on the head or shoulders of the person being ordained. The newly ordained minister will then give the closing prayer and benediction.

Ministerial Ethics

It goes without saying that a minister of the gospel should so live as to bring honor to the pastoral vocation and serve as a role model for others. But what does this generalization mean to you personally as a pastor? We must not be legalistic and overly specific, for (as Paul wrote) "the letter killeth, but the spirit giveth life" (2 Corinthians 3:6). To stimulate your thinking about a personal code of ethics, we quote in part from one suggested by a major denomination to its pastors:

Having accepted God's call to leadership in Christ's Church, I covenant with God to serve Christ and the Church with God's help, to deepen my obedience to the Two Great Commandments to love the Lord our God with all my heart, soul, mind, and strength, and to love my neighbor as myself. . . .

I will seek to support all colleagues in ministry by building constructive relationships wherever I serve, both with the staff where I work and with colleagues in neighboring churches.

I will advocate adequate compensation for my profession. I will help lay persons and colleagues to understand that professional church leaders should not expect or require fees for pastoral services from constituents they serve, when these constituents are helping pay their salaries.

I will not seek personal favors or discounts on the basis of my professional status.

I will maintain a disciplined ministry in such ways as keeping hours of prayer and devotion, endeavoring to maintain wholesome family relationships, sexual integrity, financial responsibility, regularly engaging in educational and recreational activities for professional and personal development. I will seek to maintain good health habits.

I will recognize my primary obligation to the church or employing group to which I have been called, and will accept added responsibilities only if they do not interfere with the overall effectiveness of my ministry.

I will personally and publicly support my colleagues who experience discrimination on the basis of gender, race, age, marital status, national origin, physical impairment, or disability.

I will, upon my resignation or retirement, sever my professional church leadership relations with my former constituents, and will not make professional contacts in the field of another professional church leader without his or her request and/or consent.

I will hold in confidence any privileged communication received by me during the conduct of my ministry. I will not disclose confidential communications in private or public except when in my practice of ministry I am convinced that the sanctity of confidentiality is outweighed by my well-founded belief that the parishioner/client will cause imminent, life-threatening, or substantial harm to self or others, or unless the privilege is waived by those giving the information.

I will not proselytize from other Christian churches.

I will show my personal love for God as revealed in Jesus Christ in my life and ministry, as I strive together with my colleagues to preserve the dignity, maintain the discipline, and promote the integrity of the vocation to which we have been called.[*]

---

[*]Ministers Council, American Baptist Churches in the U.S.A.

2. Preaching the Gospel

Of all the elements that go to make up the work of ministry, preaching is probably the most conspicuous. This is not to say that it is always the most important. The needs of a particular congregation at a certain period in its life can make a difference and, of course, in a large church with more than one minister, preaching is apt to be a specialty of at least one of them, but not necessarily of others. God calls us to many forms of ministry, and it is never our place to say that one calling is higher than another. The one who preaches, however, has the opportunity to make a strong impact upon the people.

What to Preach About?

It has been said that the best sermons are prepared with the Bible in one hand and the newspaper in the other. This is, of course, one of those clever half-truths that we like to quote, and although it is not to be taken literally, it does offer an element of insight. The most effective preaching brings together the Word of God with the realities of daily life. As a preacher, you are called upon to interpret, to the best of your understanding and ability, the messages God has for the people of God in today's world. Although you are not blessed with perfect wisdom, your studies have qualified you to share your views from the pulpit.

The starting point is evangelistic preaching. Again and again your sermons should follow the advice in 2 Timothy 4:5: "Do the work of an evangelist, make full proof of thy ministry." Thus, you will frequently invite the congregation to accept the invitation that Jesus offers in such texts as Matthew 11:28: "Come unto me, all ye that labor and are heavy laden, and I will give you rest." Christ's salvation is promised to all who will accept it, and your preaching delivers this message to those who hunger for it. You will do well to invite a specific response, such as coming forward during the closing hymn or in some other specific action.

Preaching that does not go beyond this point, however, is incomplete. The very next verse, Matthew 11:29, adds a responsibility to the offer of salvation: "Take my yoke upon you, and learn of me; for I am meek and lowly in heart; and ye shall find rest unto your souls." What is this yoke? Like the yoke that enables oxen to pull a load, Christ's yoke leads to a responsibility for living the Christian life. True evangelism is a call not only to the person of Christ but to Christian living as well. Therefore, in your preaching you are responsible for helping the congregation to understand and accept moral and ethical responsibilities in personal and public life that go with Christian discipleship.

Some sermons are best developed by beginning with a Bible text and exploring its implications. For instance, what do words like those of Jesus—"Blessed are the merciful, for they shall obtain mercy"—really mean when we think them through? What are some of the circumstances in daily life that call Christians to be merciful? Why is it so hard to be merciful? How do we understand the corollary about obtaining mercy—do we always receive the mercy we "deserve"? Is our reason for being merciful so that people will be merciful to us, or do we have deeper motivations? Let your imagination roam as you develop a text.

This book is designed to help you locate texts that can be effectively developed into sermons. Part II contains hundreds of selected portions of Scripture classified under topical headings that will offer suggestions for preaching. Browse among them as you select themes for your sermons.

Sometimes it is good to develop a Bible-based sermon from a larger segment of Scripture. For instance, what does an overview of Paul's letter to the Philippians tell us about the life of a church? Or what do we learn from the book of Jonah about putting our personal concerns above the will of God as we understand it? Or how does Hosea's love for his unfaithful wife help us to recognize God's love for us?

Another effective way to develop a sermon is to begin with a problem that may concern many members of your congregation. Why do good people suffer? Why don't our children sometimes turn out the way we wish? How are we to react to modern standards of sexual behavior? Why do I sometimes feel that my prayers are unanswered? How can God help me to overcome temptations? The list is endless, and there is help in the Bible if you will search for it, using such help to bring the sermon to a spiritual conclusion.

A series of related sermons can be useful. For instance, you might preach separately on each of the Ten Commandments or Beatitudes, or on several of the Old Testament prophets. These could be delivered on successive Sundays or spaced farther apart, as on second Sundays for several months.

In selecting texts, remember that the heart of the Christian faith is in the New Testament rather than the Old. There are many useful and appropriate passages in the Old Testament, however, especially in the Psalms and some of the Prophets. The key to the wise selection of Old Testament texts is to compare them with the messages of Jesus. For instance, although the doctrine of "an eye for an eye and a tooth for a tooth" appears in Exodus 21, Leviticus 24, and Deuteronomy 19, Jesus specifically rejects it in Matthew 5:38-39. Many other areas where the teachings of Christ supersede those of the Old Testament are not specifically stated, but are no less clear to the Christian preacher. When you have selected the topic for a particular sermon, give it a title that will express the main idea you want to convey. It will help not only to focus your own thinking but to fix the basic idea in the listeners' minds.

Understand the spiritual needs of your people, and speak to them.

Preparing to Preach

A good basic topic should be expressed in a well-organized fashion. Use an outline. The old dictum that a sermon should have three points is, of course, unduly arbitrary. Sometimes a single point is enough, provided that various implications are explored and helpful illustrations are used. Or you may choose to present even four or five related points. The main issue is whether you have a way of making your points clearly enough that they are remembered. Don't be afraid to repeat words for emphasis; repetition, used intentionally, can be a useful rhetorical device. A brief introductory summary at the beginning and another at the conclusion can be helpful.

Another effective device is to relate the outline to a familiar sequence such as the Ten Commandments, or to fix it in the people's minds with a particularly compelling illustration at the end or with a storytelling approach that runs through the entire sermon. Sometimes a familiar text may be broken down for discussion phrase by phrase. You will use different methods in different sermons—and you should. But the important thing is to select approaches that the congregation will remember.

It is helpful to have a unity that runs through the entire service. You can choose Scripture readings and hymns that blend with the theme of the sermon. With the cooperation of the minister of music, the service may include anthems that carry out the basic theme of the service. On special occasions some visualization can be used, such as displaying a banner, a poster, a painting, or a piece of sculpture. Stained-glass windows may also be used as visual aids.

Delivering the Message

Many a good sermon has failed to accomplish its purpose because it was poorly delivered. If you would convey your message successfully, pay attention to your style of speaking. Above all, be sure you are heard. Do not mumble or murmur. Speak loudly enough that (with or without a microphone, as the case may be) everybody, even those who cannot hear very well, will not be disappointed.

Almost as important as the volume of your voice are such qualities as the speed, the tone, and the expression. Some preachers talk too fast to be easily understood. A slow delivery is much easier to follow than a rapid flow of words, especially in a room that has echoes. A tone that is shrill or sanctimonious can discourage the listener. A delivery that drones on and on without emphasis on important points can invite drowsiness. It may help you to ask a few members of the congregation to listen critically and report back on such items as volume, speed, tone, and expression. Practice to improve your delivery and invite follow-up comments. Ask these people: Am I improving?

Some preachers prefer to preach from a manuscript, some from notes, and some without any written helps at all. There are values and dangers in each method. Which is best for you? If you use a manuscript, will you stick too closely to it, reading in a dull, monotonous voice? Or will you read expressively, looking frequently at the people, departing from the text when a new idea strikes, smiling or frowning or gazing more seriously, adjusting your tone in keeping with the content? If you use notes, will your sentences be complete and grammatical, with helpful nuances of expression to make your points effectively? If you use no helps at all, will you cover your subject in a logical and clear fashion without rambling or overlooking important emphases? Try varying your methods and determine what works best for you.

Use language that is appropriate for as many of your congregation as possible. Think of their diversity. Some may be university graduates, even with advanced degrees; others may have limited education. Some appreciate the expressions currently in favor with youth (but beware how rapidly they change!), while others prefer more traditional language. Some may have difficulty with English, using it only as a second language. After assessing your congregation's listening skills, speak in a way that your congregation will best understand and accept. The manner of your speaking can strengthen or weaken the ideas in your sermon. What will you do about it?

3. Pastoral Care

Pastoral care is one of the most important parts of your ministry. Members of your church and others in the congregation need to be aware of your concern for them. In other sections of this book we discuss the care that you as a pastor will provide on two very special occasions (the wedding and the funeral), but true pastoral care is much more comprehensive than this. It is a lifelong concern for the spiritual welfare of each person in your extended church family.

Keeping in Touch

In earlier days it was common for the pastor to make a personal call at least once or twice a year upon each member of the congregation as well as upon others who had shown an interest in the church—particularly those who might wish to make a profession of faith or bring their letter of transfer from another church. This contact was maintained by walking or driving around the neighborhood on many afternoons and some evenings and dropping in for a visit. Many circumstances make this practice less feasible nowadays, for instance, the increased employment of women, which makes them less available to receive calls; the growing concern for security from crime, which makes people more reluctant to answer unexpected rings of the doorbell; and the increasing demand on a pastor's time for other purposes, which reduces the opportunities to go calling.

What to do? You can begin by recognizing that your main objective is not to accumulate an impressive statistic for your annual report by stating how many hundred calls you made during the year, but rather to let your people know that you care about them and are available to help in time of need. Occasional friendly phone calls will help. So will repeated reminders that you will be glad to drop in (or meet them in your study) for a visit by appointment. "Can't we get together some time for a chat?" is a useful bit of conversation that may open the way for a time of sharing. Lunch dates, especially with employed persons who can spare a noontime hour or so, are a possibility. Brief personal notes (better than greeting cards) establish a bond on special occasions such as birthdays, anniversaries, engagements, graduations, promotions, retirements, illnesses, accidents, and recognitions. And just a bit of friendly, casual conversation that does not deal with church programs or issues but rather focuses on the person's other interests can show that you care.

If through any of these leads you sense that the individual is troubled about something, perhaps in church or family relationships or in personal life, a natural follow-up would be something like this: "Yes, I can see that you are concerned about this. Would you like to get together in the next few days and talk about it? When would be a good time for you?"

The deacons can be extremely helpful to you in your pastoral ministry. A diaconate that maintains a feelings in some subtle way later on, but first you must accept that they are real.

Remember that you are present as a spiritual counselor. Therefore, make use of Bible readings, devotional insights, and prayer insofar as the patient seems ready to accept these. Such conversation should be quiet and personal, never spoken in the manner of preaching to all in the room.

In the case of a person who is not expected to recover, you may be perplexed as to what to say. It may be helpful to confer with the physician and the family for guidance and understanding before counseling the person. Sometimes it is best to help the patient face the crisis ahead; on other occasions too much frankness may only make a bad situation worse.

When calling on the sick, your ministry also includes recognizing and providing the kinds of help that fellow church members can offer to the sick person. Is there a need for child care? for meals to be cooked? for help with expenses? for friendly visits? for blood donations? If so, pass the word along. In such matters you can often guide fellow church members toward helpful expressions of Christian love.

congregational care list can contribute greatly to your effectiveness in relating to the people. Ideally, each deacon will have a list of members who are his or her special responsibility, and every member will be on some deacon's list. The deacon will make a concentrated effort to maintain friendly relationships with these special people and can provide you with tips as to times when it is particularly important for you to make a personal contact.

Visiting the Shut-Ins

Persons who because of age or physical problems are confined to their homes or to special care facilities need extra attention, and you will want to visit them as often as your schedule permits. Again, the support of deacons (as well as other members of the congregation) will be a welcome addition to your own ministry. Feel free to ask such persons to visit the shut-ins, especially those with whom they can relate most comfortably.

Nothing takes the place of your own visits, however. Sensitivity on your part is the key to your effectiveness. Should you make frequent brief calls or visit less often but at greater length? It depends on the person and on the circumstances. Watch for spoken or unspoken signals as to how long you should stay. Be alert to leading remarks and body language that will indicate fatigue, pain, discouragement, frustration, or other problems. Without asking questions that the person may perceive as meddlesome or nosy, your general comments and inquiries can open the gates to helpful conversation. Sometimes just repeating or summarizing something the person has said shows that you have been listening attentively. For instance: "You say that this hasn't been one of your best days. I'm sorry to hear that." Then pause for a few moments of silence, giving the person an opportunity to respond. Although prayer can be appropriate in any pastoral call, it is particularly so when visiting shut-ins. An inspirational reading from the Bible or another source is likely to be welcome also.

Visiting the Sick

Visitation of the sick is one of your special duties as the pastor. You will find that it provides a blessing for the patient and that you in return will be blessed. It is not always easy to be aware of sickness in the congregation, and yet people will expect you to know. Therefore, you will do well to remind the church members from time to time of your desire to be informed about their own illnesses and those of others. Some hospitals will notify you when one of your church members is admitted, and many of them maintain a file that you can consult for familiar

names or church preferences. Don't overlook suc\ opportunities to become informed.

As a pastor, you will usually have the privilege c making hospital calls outside of regular visitin\ hours. Use good judgment in taking advantage of th\ opportunity. "Outside of visiting hours" may be, i fact, the best time to call because it can provide mo\ privacy for serious conversation than when oth\ visitors are present. Furthermore, it seems somewh\ unfair to usurp a time when the patient's family a\ friends can visit. Be ready, however, to yield to ba\ time, treatment time, doctors' calls, baby-feedi\ time, and perhaps also meal time. Most calls on t\ sick should be brief so as not to tire the patients, \ there can be occasions when they would prefe\ longer visit to allow time for discussing special c\ cerns. Your sensitivity to each patient's partic\ needs is valuable.

Your manner when making a sick call is im\ tant. Try to be warm and understanding, sympat\ and pleasantly cheerful—never boisterous, lou\ gumentative, critical of the doctor or hospit\ pessimistic about the patient's symptoms. Neve\ less, if the patient wants to say something cr\ discouraged, or bitter, you need to be a willin\ tener, recognizing the fact that this is the wa\ person feels. You may be able to counteract

Pastoral Counseling

It is almost impossible to be the pastor of a church and not be called upon to do at least a minimum of counseling. But why should you not want to counsel your people? It is a valuable part of ministry. It provides help to those persons who may need it most. Yet, there are some cautions.

First of all, you will need to recognize that pastoral counseling involves much more than just answering a few "What shall I do?" questions. Sometimes a person seeking help merely wants *information* that is relevant to his or her problem. More often, however, the need is for *understanding* or *insight*, which may require many sessions, in which the counselor dispenses a minimum of advice but encourages the person to work out his or her own problem through conversation with the spiritual counselor. These two approaches are called *directive* and *nondirective* counseling respectively.

As an insightful pastor, you will presumably be able to recognize problems that you do not feel qualified to deal with or do not have the time to discuss adequately over the many hours of meeting that will be needed. In such cases you may need to refer the person to a professional counselor, but there is value in your continuing involvement by discussing the situation from time to time with the professional and providing such helpful support as the two of you can agree upon.

A necessary caution in these times when charges of harassment are not uncommon is to be particularly careful in counseling a person of the opposite sex to avoid any intimacy or even the appearance of intimacy that can be misunderstood. Obviously, counseling requires a degree of privacy if it is to be effective, and therefore you are required to walk a narrow line. There is no firm rule for your protection and that of your counselee, but it may be helpful at least to have another person outside your closed door who would be aware of any loud threats or protests.

Bear in mind the importance of confidentiality in counseling. Those who come to you with questions and problems will feel able to discuss them freely with you only if they are sure you will not betray their trust. They should feel assured that the information they reveal in confidence to their pastoral counselor is privileged material which will not be passed on to others. Unfortunately, not everybody respects this confidentiality, and some people may pressure you to share such material with them. It is wise to resist such approaches firmly, not only to keep faith with your counselee but to protect yourself from a reputation for indiscriminate sharing of information, which may impair future counseling relationships with others.

A means of maximizing your pastoral counseling skills is available through programs of Clinical Pastoral Education (CPE). These are offered by most theological seminaries and by many institutions in which counseling is done, such as hospitals, retirement communities, and large nursing homes. They customarily include not only textbook study but also actual practice in counseling, supervised by experienced counselors. The Association for Clinical Pastoral Education, Inc., an organization that accredits such programs, defines CPE this way:

> Clinical Pastoral Education is a method of theological education where a student learns pastoral skills within the context of responsible relationships to people under the direct supervision of a trained clergy person. It provides a learning situation for a theological student and continuing education for clergy in which they may develop awareness of the theological and psychological concerns of persons in crisis. CPE also confronts the person with the human predicament. It supplies the nurturing milieu in which to understand the self as a person, to know the self as a pastor, to integrate one's theology more meaningfully with life, and to become aware of human worth and

potential. (From *The Standards*, Association for Clinical Pastoral Education, Inc., Decatur, Georgia, 1993.)

If you choose to participate in this kind of training, you would be well advised to select a program that is favorably recognized by this association or by the American Association of Pastoral Counselors, the Association of Marriage and Family Therapists, or the Association of Licensed Counselors.

Counseling, if done in accordance with high professional and ethical standards, can be one of the most important parts of your ministry. Not only can it help the individuals with whom you work, but it will assist you in understanding your people's spiritual needs. Thus it will enrich not only your preaching but virtually all phases of your ministry.

4. Weddings

Changing times have brought changing views of the marriage relationship to many people, but the biblical witness as stated in Matthew 5:27-28 and 31-32 clearly identifies it as the lifelong commitment of one man and one woman to each other. This view does not condone easy divorce, extramarital affairs, or couples living together without marriage.

No book can give you clear direction to cover every situation in which you are called upon to decide what couples you will accept for marriage, but some guidance is possible. Where divorced persons are concerned, what can you learn about the reasons for previous divorce? about a pattern of several divorces, indicating a casual view of marriage? about the degree of commitment between the two persons who have come to you? Where marriage of persons who have been living together unmarried is concerned, what is their understanding of the meaning of their past relationship and their future life together? It is impossible for any of us to understand fully the regrets of others over their past sins or errors and their hopes for the future, but we can try, remembering Jesus' words to a troubled woman in John 8:11: "Neither do I condemn thee: go, and sin no more."

Marriage is both a civil and a religious institution, and we of the Christian ministry represent both the state and Almighty God when we conduct a wedding. This rare combination of church-state relationship is justified by the fact that the state does not *require* that a member of the clergy perform the marriage but does *permit* such a person to do so. You will need to be familiar with the requirements of both roles.

The Minister as Representative of the State

Marriage as a civil contract consists in the parties making a declaration before competent witnesses that they take each other as husband and wife, pledging themselves to a faithful and lifelong discharge of the responsibilities reciprocally involved in that relationship. The persons designated by law to assist them in formalizing this contract and to issue a certificate that records it (in other words, to conduct the wedding and issue a certificate of marriage) are regularly ordained and recognized clergy of all denominations and certain specified civil authorities.

When you establish your residence in a particular state, either as pastor of a church or in some other form of ministry, it is important that you understand the state's requirements about marriages. Every state has its own rules and regulations, and therefore no generalizations can be made in a book like this. Information can usually be obtained from the secretary of state in your state capital or possibly from the regional office of your denomination. Are you authorized to perform marriages? If you are the ordained pastor of a local church, there is very little doubt that you are. But what if you are a minister without a church? What if you are licensed, but not ordained? To be certain, get the facts.

It is also essential that you understand fully your state's requirements concerning marriage licenses. Is there a time limit of any kind on their use? Are there restrictions as to where in the state a particular license can be used? Are there legal requirements about the signatures (including those of witnesses) that must appear on the certificate of marriage or about how promptly it must be returned?

Insist on having the marriage license in your hands before the wedding takes place, and examine it carefully to be sure it is valid for the intended use. Under no circumstances should you conduct a wedding upon the promise that a license will be delivered or that an invalid one will be corrected. To do so may create serious legal problems both for you and for the couple.

It is reasonable to assume that the office that issued the license has checked on the eligibility of the persons coming to be married, but if you have serious reason to suspect any irregularity (for instance, whether the persons are of legal age, whether they are both presently unmarried, or whether they are mentally and physically competent), you should satisfy these doubts before continuing with the wedding.

Counseling with the Couple

You will want to meet in advance, possibly several times, with the couple who plan to be married. The most obvious part of these sessions is to exchange some basic information about the forthcoming event. The couple will use this opportunity to share with you any ideas they may have about the ceremony, and you in turn will be able to inform them about the requirements of the state and of your church. Together, then, the three of you can do some basic planning for the wedding day.

There is more than this to be considered in these discussions together, however. You, and presumably they as well, are concerned that theirs will be a happy and stable marriage. You are not just taking part in what is to be a beautiful ceremony; you are participating in the creation of a new family unit. Some heart-to-heart conversations about the nature of marriage and family life are therefore in order as you take this opportunity to offer counseling, especially on subjects where marital troubles are apt to arise. Some leading questions that you might ask them are these. You will probably think of others.

—Why do you want to be married to each other?

—What kind of commitment are you ready to make?

—What do such traditional phrases as "for richer or poorer," "in sickness and in health," and "so long as we both shall live" mean to you?

—What do you think are some of the requirements for a stable marriage?

—How do you know that you are really in love?

—How does each of you feel about having children? Do you have similar views on family planning?

—What thought have you given to managing your finances together? Will you share everything, or do you intend to have a prenuptial agreement?

—How do you get along with your own and your partner's family?

—Have you discussed with each other any health problems you may have?

—Are there physical aspects of the marriage relationship that you need to talk about with a counselor?

—Where will you live—in a home of your own or one shared with others?

—How do you plan to share your spiritual life?

Questions such as these are not intended as an interrogation but rather as an opportunity to open discussions. Be sensitive to the couple's responses and pursue the discussions only if you can do so without intruding in areas that they clearly would rather not talk about. Your mission is to be helpful to the extent that help is welcomed.

The Wedding Rehearsal

If the wedding is to be at all formal, a rehearsal is not only useful but almost essential. Insist that every participant be present if it is humanly possible.

You should receive the license at the rehearsal. If signatures of official witnesses will be needed on the certificate, be sure you and they know who has this responsibility (usually the best man and maid or matron of honor). They need to understand when and where after the ceremony they will meet you to perform that important task.

Discuss with the ushers what they are expected to do. What seats will they reserve for families of the bride and groom? Will they strictly observe the "bride's side, groom's side" pattern of seating the guests, or will they lead people to the best available locations? Will ushers offer an arm to women guests in escorting them to their seats? Where and when and by whom will the parents be seated? Will all ushers participate in the bridal procession, or will one or two remain in the rear to respond to any emergencies? Will ushers be responsible for checking on details such as heat, light, air conditioning, or ventilation?

A well-planned and organized bridal procession is important to set the tone for a formal wedding. You can insure this by helping all members of the wedding party to understand at the rehearsal what is expected of them. They need to know when and in what order they will enter, how much space to allow between the various persons, and even what kind of steps they will take. Practice the processional, preferably with music.

Be sure there is a clear understanding as to who will carry the rings and how the rings can be readily accessible when they are needed. If a child is to serve as ring bearer, how can the rings be protected from accidental dropping and yet be readily available at the proper time?

The entire ceremony should be read at the rehearsal, not only to remind the couple of the commitment they are making, but to be sure they understand when they must speak and what they should say. They should rehearse the actual words they are to say. If you do not at this time pronounce that they are husband and wife, there will be no confusion about when the marriage actually occurred.

Also at the rehearsal you should be sure wedding party members know exactly where they will stand during the ceremony and in what order they will leave for the recessional; also, who will participate in the receiving line and where.

The Wedding Ceremony

As a pastor you are responsible for the tone of a Christian wedding. Your own personality and manner will play an important part. It should be cheerful, joyous, and inspiring, without sacrificing the dignity and reverence of a worship service. The actual form of the ceremony may vary. Some appropriate marriage services are found in Part III of this book, but there is no reason why creative pastors should not develop their own. Some pastors like to include a brief homily on the meaning of marriage in their wedding ceremony. Some possible texts for this appear in the section on marriage in Part II of this book.

Some couples like to write their own marriage services, and this can be an excellent shared experience if with your help they give careful thought to the nature of the promises they plan to make before God and the atmosphere of commitment and inspiration that will be created for themselves and for others present. Help them to think through the implications of words, phrases, and quotations that they would like to include.

Where should the wedding be held? Ideally in the church sanctuary or a chapel, where the surroundings testify to the presence of God in this act of mutual dedication. As the officiating minister, you can often influence this choice. If other locations are being considered, you may be able to help the couple to think about their appropriateness by asking such questions as these: "How will this setting help to create an awareness of God's presence?" and "What special meaning does this have for you that will emphasize the commitments you are making to each other?" Such discussion may aid in making a decision between a home or garden and a restaurant or night club.

You as the officiating minister may appropriately exercise full authority in the actual conduct of the service. You will want to give due consideration to the wishes of the participants, especially the bride. Some couples will emphasize traditionalism, others creativity, and either may be suitable in a particular wedding, but it is your part to guide participants tactfully away from that which is irreverent or in bad taste. Your position may require you to mediate in disputes involving others such as the bride's mother or a wedding consultant. Although your authority does not extend to the reception (except in the enforcement of church regulations), it is very considerable as it relates to the ceremony itself.

The Reception

Your role at the reception may be quite limited. If the couple has been encouraged to have this event at the church (and what could be more appropriate?), you may be the church's representative, the cordial host, seeing to it that the needs of the guests are met, but at the same time insuring that the wedding party understands what is or is not appropriate in that setting.

What about the use of alcoholic beverages at the reception? If it is held on church property, the congregation or a responsible church board should establish and enforce a clear policy in the matter, thus relieving you of making arbitrary rules on the spot. If the reception is held in a location where there are no restrictions on alcohol use, the decision is up to the couple involved. You as the minister are free to bear your witness, if you wish, by courteously turning down the offered beverage or declining to attend the reception.

After the Wedding Is Over

Your relationship with the couple you have united in marriage goes on. Call on them after they have established a home and support them in any way you can. Let them know that you are available to discuss any concerns they may have and that the church welcomes them as full participants in its life. If they have never become Christians, there would be no better step for them to take as they embark on life together.

5. Funerals

Your ministry to those who have been separated by death from their loved ones is another of your most significant pastoral responsibilities. It begins at or before the moment when you hear that death has occurred and continues for several weeks or even longer. It is a rich opportunity for serving families, both before and after the funeral as well as in the service itself.

Preparation for Death

Death comes to all of us eventually, sometimes suddenly with little or no warning, other times at the end of a long and serious illness. It has been said, in fact, that death is a normal part of life. As pastor, it is your privilege to prepare the people of your congregation for this great transition by including in your preaching from time to time the promise of Christ that his people shall inherit eternal life. Equally appropriate are informal discussions about the nature of the funeral or memorial service, considering together with the individual's family what it is appropriate to include and why.

Personal counseling also offers opportunities to talk about death, especially with older persons, those who are chronically or terminally ill, or their families and close friends. Here, as in most counseling situations, it is important to be a good listener. Tune your hearing to recognize hints that the person wants to talk about the end of life, and allow him or her to do so. Sometimes a very general question such as "How do you feel about what's ahead for you?" will encourage the person to respond with a remark that initiates a helpful discussion. But a more blunt approach may create morbid fears that would inhibit a sick person's recovery. Sensitivity is the key.

The Setting for the Funeral Service

Most funerals are conducted either in the funeral home or in some special area of the church building, such as the sanctuary or a chapel. Although a private home is not inappropriate, it creates an unnecessary disruption for families that are already heavily burdened. The funeral home offers a comfortable atmosphere for visiting hours and is suitable for funerals of persons who do not have close ties with the church. For church members and others who feel especially close to the congregation, however, there is no better location in which to hold the funeral than the church itself. As pastor, you have the privilege to encourage its use for funerals by those for whom it is appropriate. You can remind the congregation of this option from time to time, and when occasion arises, you can specifically invite individual church families to use the building in this way. Use begets use, and each funeral held there provides encouragement for others to follow suit.

Meeting with the Family

If the person who has died has been seriously ill for some time, you have probably already established a link with the family before death occurs, and you may have discussed with them some of the arrangements that will need to be made. It may be, however, that death has come suddenly or that you have been contacted after the fact by the funeral director on behalf of relatives unrelated to the church. In either case you should establish communication with the family promptly so as to offer sympathy and comfort as well as any counseling they may require.

Although a call at the funeral parlor during visiting hours is never inappropriate, a call at the family home offers more opportunity for private conversation and prayer. It is often advisable to telephone in advance and make this visit by appointment. At this time it may be possible to discuss details of the service, although in some cases the emotional state of the family may suggest postponing this discussion until the following day.

The relationship with the family does not end with

the funeral. Sometimes there is a shared meal after the service, and if you are invited, the family will appreciate your acceptance. This event is a first step in the healing process, and your presence can be helpful.

In the days that follow, you will want to regard this family as rather "special." Make a point of visiting or telephoning occasionally and offering help with practical or spiritual matters that may be troubling them. But don't make a nuisance of yourself.

Recognize, with the writer of Ecclesiastes, that "there is a time to keep silence and a time to speak." Again, sensitivity is all-important.

The Funeral Service

Although pastors of those denominations that have a prescribed liturgy will follow it rather closely, others will plan a service that seems appropriate to them in the particular situation. There is no fixed order of service for a funeral. A common order for a relatively brief service is this: a reading of selected portions of Scripture; the reading of appropriate quotations or prose or poetry; some remarks or a brief address that closes with a rather personal prayer of thankfulness for the life of the person who has died; and a benediction. Some may wish also to open with prayer. (Further suggestions appear in Part IV of this book.)

You may select appropriate Scriptures for use in various ways during the funeral from several of the collections included in Part II of this book. Look especially under the following headings: Faith and Trust in God, Prayer and Supplication, Good Works, Children and Youth, Readings for the Sick and Shut-In, Death and Eternal Life, Grief, Comfort, the Cross of Christ, and the Resurrection of Christ.

Organ music before and after the service is appropriate, and this is often available in funeral homes. Many services that are held in church settings include one or more hymns chosen to fit the personality and interests of the person being remembered or to express the sense of Christian triumph that transcends the grief of separation.

Although funeral services are usually kept rather brief, sometimes there are reasons to extend them by providing for personal tributes. A few friends, family members, or associates may be invited to speak briefly about their memories. We have even participated in services where anyone present who wished to speak briefly was free to do so, and this was a very moving experience. Each funeral service that you plan is a creation of its own, designed to be as appropriate as possible to the memory of the person being honored and to the spiritual needs of the family.

Opinions differ as to whether the body of the deceased person should be displayed during the funeral service. Especially in a church setting, an open casket tends to detract from the positive emphasis on immortal life that should characterize the Christian funeral. Yet, psychologically, some people need to view the body in order to say goodbye. If there have been calling hours at the funeral home prior to the service, there may be no advantage in having the casket open at all at the church. An acceptable compromise, either at the funeral home or at church, is to have the casket open for a time before the service but closed before the funeral begins.

Funerals Involving Unusual Circumstances

Some funerals are particularly difficult for all concerned, including the officiating minister. Among these are the death of an infant or child or of the victim of an accident or disaster or of a young adult whose life seemed to offer unusual promise. In such circumstances many will have in their minds the eternal question "Why does death come in this way to people who do not seem ready for it?" As you conduct the service, you will need to keep this question in mind, even though you may not be able to answer it any more precisely than Job could understand the reason for his torment. This is not the time for theological discourse on why bad things happen to good people, but rather for comfort through the message that is appropriate in all circumstances and all theologies: God cares.

Possibly you may be asked to officiate at the funeral of a person who has committed suicide. How do you deal with this situation in the service? It would be wrong to ignore the circumstances of death. You might refer sympathetically to the tortured feelings that would drive a person to such an extreme act and point out that many of us, though we have never turned to suicide, have also had feelings of desperation. This is an occasion to remind others that as Christians, we must rededicate ourselves to "bear...one another's burdens, and so fulfil the law of Christ" (Galatians 6:2).

A funeral for a person who has been particularly prominent in the church or community offers an opportunity for a somewhat more complex service than usual, with brief tributes by various persons particularly qualified to give them.

The Burial

After the service there may be a funeral procession to the cemetery. The minister will usually preside at the graveside service, which may consist of a short prayer, a sentence of committal or very brief remarks, and a benediction. In many communities it is customary for the minister to walk in front of the casket when it is being carried to the hearse or to the grave site.

If the burial is held in a distant location, the family may spare the local minister the trip, either by having the committal immediately after the funeral and at the same location or by arranging for another minister who lives in the vicinity of the cemetery to meet the funeral cars there for a graveside service.

Memorial Services

In some congregations there is a growing trend toward holding a memorial service instead of a funeral. There may be various reasons for choosing this option, such as cremation of the body, donation of organs, a preference for speedy burial, or a desire to postpone the service until more friends or family can be present. A memorial service at a convenient time such as a weekend hour is a particularly good choice if many of those who would like to attend are employed and would have difficulty doing so at an earlier time.

Since no casket is present at a memorial service, it may be held several days or even a few weeks after the death, thus allowing more time for planning it. It thus affords more opportunity than a funeral for participation by family and friends, as the passage of time has made it less painful to speak of memories and feelings. A memorial service would normally be held in the church sanctuary and would include many of the elements of a funeral but would be designed more in the style of a normal congregational worship service, including congregational singing and perhaps other ingredients such as responsive readings and anthems.

6. Church Administration

Many pastors brush aside church administration as an unimportant part of their ministry, while others go to the opposite extreme. Unless you are called to a very large church with multiple staff, however, you really cannot afford to disregard any part of your ministry, nor for that matter to overemphasize any to the neglect of others. When the apostle Paul wrote about spiritual gifts in 1 Corinthians 12, he reminded the church that no part of Christian ministry is unimportant and no spiritual gift is less significant than any other. Take church administration seriously, but don't let it dominate your ministry!

Patterns of Organization in Local Churches

Most churches have several boards or committees that are responsible for various parts of their ministry, as well as some kind of overall body that coordinates their efforts. Some are "one board" structures, in which a single board or council administers the work of the church with authority to act in most matters when the congregation is not in session. Normally these have several subsidiary boards or committees that divide up the responsibilities for administration. The more traditional "multiple board" model provides a greater degree of authority for the individual boards than the "one board" form, but it coordinates them through a church council that consists of board chairpersons and certain other church officers.

Whichever pattern is used, there is usually a church moderator or lay leader, who presides over the council and the meetings of the congregation. In some churches the pastor serves as moderator, but more often this is an elected lay person.

As pastor you need to be an active participant in all of these boards or committees as well as in the overall board or council. Whether you have a vote or not is unimportant. If you can influence church policies only by casting the deciding vote on a closely debated issue, you will win a shallow victory. Your strongest power is persuasion, and this is helped by a willingness to compromise when Christian principle is not at issue. Of course you need to be present and ready to speak on appropriate occasions in board meetings. Obviously, to do this you need to know what is going on and why. But this is a matter of making your presence known, not of casting a vote.

Don't allow yourself to become a demagogue or a dictator. Speak out when your conscience bids you to do so, but hold your tongue when you can. Your influence will be greater if you do not squander it. The pastor is not the boss of the church, but the spiritual leader. Jesus' advice to the twelve to be "wise as serpents and harmless as doves" may stand you in good stead.

Spiritual Life in the Church

A board of deacons (or diaconate) is present in almost every church, occasionally under some other name. This body is responsible for administering the spiritual life of the church. Ideally it should be a group of deeply dedicated, friendly, outgoing Christians who care about all of God's people—not only the members of this church, not only the committed Christians of this world, but all of God's people.

In some churches the deacons' work is simplified to the point where they do little more than prepare and serve Communion, assist the pastor with baptismal services, and administer a fellowship fund for financial aid to the needy. Although these are essential functions, they fall far short of the deacons' basic responsibility to strengthen the spiritual life of Christ's church.

Congregational care is a particularly important responsibility. Each deacon should have several members assigned for personal watchcare. The deacon should be ready to respond in any area of life, but especially in case of sickness, family problems, death of loved ones, or times of special joy, offering Christian friendship and support and notifying the minister when there is a particular need for pastoral care.

Newcomers are another special concern of deacons. Although all members of the church should be ready to greet visitors warmly, deacons can make this a special effort. They can show the visitors around the building, introduce them to people they might find congenial, guide them to seats in the worship service, help them and their children to find Sunday school classes, and invite the family to fellowship hour, if there is one. They can involve members in visitation programs to extend the church's invitation to others. And when persons respond to the invitation for decision and membership, the deacons can interview them, not sternly like watchdogs at the gate, but in the mood of welcome and encouragement: "How can we help you to find a place in our fellowship?"

Deacons have a ministry to the pastor also. A pastoral relations committee that meets confidentially with you to discuss mutual concerns, both joys and problems, can be an effective force in strengthening the ties that bind. Such a committee does not have to be a function of the diaconate; it can be a separate entity of the church, but the diaconate is a logical place for it. The basic principle of such a committee must be that pastor and people come together to ask "How can we find ways to work more effectively for the advancement of Christ's kingdom?"

Other matters that affect the spiritual life of the church may be included in the responsibilities of the diaconate itself or in committees working under the deacons' guidance. Following is a listing of such committees.

Evangelistic outreach: Every church needs to enrich its spiritual life through some form of outreach to bring persons to a confession of Christian faith and baptism or to the transfer of their letter from another church when they move into your community. There are many forms of evangelism, such as preaching, home visitation, letter writing, telephoning, fellowship groups, and distribution of literature. The important part is that the church have some method of extending Christ's call to others. Whether the deacons accept this role themselves or take steps to see that it happens through others, they are concerned that in some way it gets done.

Social concern: This is another aspect of the spiritual life of the church. In a democratic society this is especially true. Citizens have not only the privilege but the responsibility of influencing public policy through federal, state, and municipal legislators they elect. As citizens of a democracy, our various levels of government are not *they*; our government is *we*. Without involving the church in politics, Christians can express their individual convictions on public morality and ethics in the political arena, even if they do not agree with those of their brother or sister in the next pew. Like the prophet Amos, we need not shrink from matters of right and wrong in government.

Missions: This is a combination of some elements of evangelism and social concern. Jesus was not only concerned that we share the gospel with our neighbors, but in the Great Commission he has called us to go into all the world, preaching the gospel and baptizing. Does your church adequately support your denomination's missionary outreach and a few selected social service programs in your community?

Where in your church does the responsibility lie for developing an awareness among the members of the church's mission in the world? Who takes responsibility for telling people about churches, hospitals, agricultural stations, schools, and other Christian enterprises half a world away, or ministries with children, the elderly, the homeless, the underprivileged, or those newly arrived from other lands who need us and perhaps live within half an hour's drive of our homes? Surely they are part of our spiritual concern and responsibility.

Church music: Here is another area of spiritual life in the church. Have you never been moved spiritually by an inspiring anthem or by a beautiful prelude? Here again is an area for concern on the part of the diaconate. The music committee may or may not be part of the deacons' responsibility, but the deacons' caring can be the motivation that leads to a deeply spiritual ministry of music.

A special concern for the music committee: In most cases it is illegal to photocopy words and music for choir or congregational use without obtaining permission from the copyright holder. Usually a phone call or letter to the publisher will provide the needed information.

Hospitality: Even the serving of food can be spiritual. For Jesus, dining with his disciples was a spiritual experience. Worshipers in the apostolic churches shared fellowship meals, sometimes even love feasts. The sharing of a meal can be a spiritual experience in your church, and there is a spiritual aura around the work of the kitchen committee that is very real but that is not often recognized. Again, the deacons have good reason to care about this part of the church's spiritual life, and perhaps even to include it under their responsibilities.

As you can see, this is not just a catalog of duties of the diaconate but rather suggestions of many areas of service that will be a significant part of the spiritual ministry in many churches, whether conducted under the auspices of the deacons or through some independent committee. And these are all part of your ministry as pastor, not necessarily to demand your deep involvement, but to call for your care, your concern, your prayers, your understanding, and your support.

Finance and Property

Most churches manage their temporal affairs through one or more boards or committees that are separate from those that deal with spiritual matters, though ideally there is coordination through the church council so that neither loses sight of the other's concerns. In some churches a board of trustees may be responsible for all temporal matters; in others there may be more than one body with these responsibilities.

There was a time in many states when church properties were customarily owned by societies that were separate organizations that were not part of the church. Although often the society officers were church members, they were not necessarily so. Thus, at times the two organizations had differing objectives, with the possibility of considerable embarrassment to the church. If perchance your church has this archaic arrangement, it should arrange to assume legal ownership of the building in which it meets, teaches, and worships.

In many churches the title is held by a board of trustees elected by the congregation. In some situations these trustees have many responsibilities related to the church's financial affairs and property management; in others the trustees are nominal owners, and the broader responsibilities are conducted by a separate board. One can argue that the property will be better managed by a board that holds title to it than by one that does not.

Some states have legal requirements governing religious organizations. Ordinarily these are designed to protect the congregation's rights of ownership and use and do not impair the freedom of religion that the United States Constitution guarantees. It is important, however, to be aware of laws governing religious organizations. Find out what, if any, such laws exist in your state and keep a copy available for reference.

In most churches the responsibilities for business matters are centered in a single board or committee known by some title such as the board of trustees, the board of finance and property, or the finance committee. Such a body develops and recommends to the church for adoption an annual budget, continuing to watch over its implementation to ensure proper administration and accountability. It should see that all persons handling church finances are bonded and that accurate financial reports are made to the congregation. It should arrange for an annual audit of church finances. The same board or committee is responsible for the protection, management, and upkeep of church property.

The importance of systematic and orderly financial planning cannot be overemphasized. A proposed budget should be prepared in consultation with all church units that incur expenses, and this proposal should include all anticipated expenditures, including a fair share (at least a tithe) for missions. Following a solicitation of members for pledges, the budget should be adjusted if necessary before submission to the congregation for adoption. Members should be encouraged to pledge specific amounts of financial support in order to provide a reasonable basis for estimating income in the budget.

Opinions differ as to who should be responsible for the annual financial canvass. In some churches this is a responsibility of the same board or committee that administers the church's business operations. Others prefer a separate canvass committee, which has the advantage of enlisting persons with a variety of interests and responsibilities not only in promoting the solicitation of pledges but often in budget building as well.

In dealing with church finances, it is important to break away from a strictly business line of thinking. The stewardship of members' personal funds is not just a solicitation to guarantee that the bills will get paid; it is an invitation to Christian people to share the resources that God has entrusted to them as they give thanks for God's care. As Paul advised the Corinthians, "Upon the first day of the week let every one of you lay by him in store, as God hath prospered him." For many, this response is expressed through the Old Testament principle of tithing. You can provide support in your sermons at canvass time and at other points in the year, by preaching on Christian stewardship, not only of money but of time and talents as well.

As the pastor, you are not necessarily deeply involved with church business, but you need to be well informed and ready to state your position when you feel that principles are at stake. For example, if you feel that maintenance is being seriously neglected or that finances are in a precarious condition, you have a responsibility to share your views with the appropriate board. On the other hand, if you feel that too much of an emphasis is being placed on "practical" business matters to the detriment of the Sunday school, the church's missionary interests, the music and worship, or other areas that are at the center of what the church is all about, speak up!

The Church's Educational Program

The church's educational work is vitally important. Not only the Sunday school, but other forms of religious education such as the vacation school, the Sunday evening fellowship groups, after-school classes, midweek Bible study groups, senior groups, church-sponsored nursery schools, and Christian academies can all have their place in church life, varying of course with the needs of the particular congregation and community. Schools, whether they are Sunday schools or some form of weekday Christian education, should belong to the church. They should be supported by and under the control of the church. Although the church should not needlessly interfere in the details of their operations, it should maintain the right to general management. The usual way to accomplish this relationship is through a board of Christian education, to which the various educational activities report.

Although you cannot always participate as extensively in all of these activities as you or others might wish, it is essential that you take a deep interest in them and be as well informed as possible. If your church has a board of Christian education, you can participate regularly in its discussions and decisions. Attend workers' conferences as regularly as your schedule permits, and be available to provide instruction there whenever needed, especially in the areas of Bible and theology. You are a "teacher of teachers."

There are other ways in which you can relate effectively to the educational program. One is to visit the parents of the pupils in their homes, securing if possible their active participation in the worship and work of the church. Another is to teach an occasional elective course in a specialized area or to visit various classes for one or a few sessions of instruction on subjects that you feel especially well qualified to teach. Still another is to support Christian education in the Sunday morning service by special recognition of teachers and pupil promotions, by seasonal emphases, and by using the pulpit for instructional sermons on Bible themes. Take the church's educational program seriously, and let its leaders know that you care—even if your church has a separate minister of education. You, as pastor, are an important link with this vital church function.

II

Selections from the Sacred Scriptures

II

Selections from the Sacred Scriptures

Praise and Thanksgiving

O Lord our Lord, how excellent is thy name in all the earth! who hast set thy glory above the heavens. Out of the mouth of babes and sucklings hast thou ordained strength because of thine enemies, that thou mightest still the enemy and the avenger. When I consider thy heavens, the work of thy fingers, the moon and the stars, which thou hast ordained; what is man, that thou art mindful of him? and the son of man, that thou visitest him? *(Psalm 8:1-4)*

O clap your hands, all ye people; shout unto God with the voice of triumph. . . . Sing praises to God, sing praises: sing praises unto our King, sing praises. For God is the king of all the earth: sing ye praises with understanding. *(Psalm 47:1,6-7)*

Praise waiteth for thee, O God, in Zion: and unto

thee shall the vow be performed. O thou that hearest prayer, unto thee shall all flesh come. . . . We shall be satisfied with the goodness of thy house, even of thy holy temple. *(Psalm 65:1,2,4)*

Make a joyful noise unto God, all ye lands: Sing forth the honor of his name: make his praise glorious. Say unto God, How terrible art thou in thy works! through the greatness of thy power shall thine enemies submit themselves unto thee. All the earth shall worship thee, and shall sing unto thee; they shall sing to thy name. *(Psalm 66:1-4)*

Let the people praise thee, O God; let all the people praise thee. O let the nations be glad and sing for joy: for thou shalt judge the people righteously, and govern the nations upon earth. Let the people praise thee, O God; let all the people praise thee. Then shall the earth yield her increase; and God, even our own God, shall bless us. God shall bless us; and all the ends of the earth shall fear him. *(Psalm 67:3-7)*

O come, let us sing unto the Lord: let us make a joyful noise to the rock of our salvation. Let us come before his presence with thanksgiving, and make a joyful noise unto him with psalms. For the Lord is a great God, and a great King above all gods. In his hand are the deep places of the earth: the strength of the hills is his also. The sea is his, and he made it:

and his hands formed the dry land. O come, let us worship and bow down: let us kneel before the Lord our maker. For he is our God, and we are the people of his pasture, and the sheep of his hand. *(Psalm 95:1-7)*

O sing unto the Lord a new song: sing unto the Lord, all the earth. Sing unto the Lord, bless his name; show forth his salvation from day to day. Declare his glory among the heathen, his wonders among all people. For the Lord is great, and greatly to be praised: he is to be feared above all gods. For all the gods of the nations are idols: but the Lord made the heavens. Honor and majesty are before him: strength and beauty are in his sanctuary. Give unto the Lord, O ye kindreds of the people, give unto the Lord glory and strength. Give unto the Lord the glory due unto his name: bring an offering, and come into his courts. *(Psalm 96:1-8)*

O worship the Lord in the beauty of holiness: fear before him, all the earth. Say among the heathen that the Lord reigneth; the world also shall be established that it shall not be moved: he shall judge the people righteously. Let the heavens rejoice, and let the earth be glad; let the sea roar, and the fulness thereof. Let the field be joyful, and all that is therein: then shall all the trees of the wood rejoice before the Lord; for he cometh, for he cometh to judge the earth; he shall judge the world with righteousness, and the people with his truth. *(Psalm 96:9-13)*

O sing unto the Lord a new song; for he hath done marvelous things: his right hand, and his holy arm, hath gotten him the victory. The Lord hath made known his salvation: his righteousness hath he openly showed in the sight of the heathen. He hath remembered his mercy and his truth toward the house of Israel: all the ends of the earth have seen the salvation of our God. Make a joyful noise unto the Lord, all the earth: make a loud noise, and rejoice, and sing praise. *(Psalm 98:1-4)*

Sing unto the Lord with the harp; with the harp, and the voice of a psalm. With trumpets and sound of cornet make a joyful noise before the Lord, the King. Let the sea roar, and the fulness thereof; the world, and they that dwell therein. Let the floods clap their hands: let the hills be joyful together before the Lord; for he cometh to judge the earth: with righteousness shall he judge the world, and the people with equity. *(Psalm 98:5-9)*

O God, my heart is fixed; I will sing and give praise, even with my glory. Awake, psaltery and harp: I myself will awake early. I will praise thee, O Lord, among the people: and I will sing praises unto thee among the nations. For thy mercy is great above the heavens: and thy truth reacheth unto the clouds. Be thou exalted, O God, above the heavens: and thy glory above all the earth; that thy beloved may be delivered: save with thy right hand, and answer me. *(Psalm 108:1-6)*

I will praise thee with my whole heart: before the gods will I sing praise unto thee. I will worship toward thy holy temple, and praise thy name for thy lovingkindness and for thy truth: for thou hast magnified thy word above all thy name. In the day when I cried, thou answeredst me, and strengthenedst me with strength in my soul. All the kings of the earth shall praise thee, O Lord, when they hear the words of thy mouth. Yea, they shall sing in the ways of the Lord: for great is the glory of the Lord. *(Psalm 138:1-5)*

I will extol thee, my God, O King; and I will bless thy name for ever and ever. Every day will I bless thee; and I will praise thy name for ever and ever. Great is the Lord, and greatly to be praised; and his greatness is unsearchable. One generation shall praise thy works to another, and shall declare thy mighty acts. I will speak of the glorious honor of thy majesty, and of thy wondrous works. *(Psalm 145:1-5)*

Praise ye the Lord: for it is good to sing praises unto our God; for it is pleasant, and praise is comely.

The Lord doth build up Jerusalem: he gathereth together the outcasts of Israel. He healeth the broken in heart, and bindeth up their wounds. *(Psalm 147:1-3)*

Praise ye the Lord. Sing unto the Lord a new song and his praise in the congregation of saints. Let Israel rejoice in him that made him: let the children of Zion be joyful in their King. Let them praise his name in the dance: let them sing praises unto him with the timbrel and harp. For the Lord taketh pleasure in his people. *(Psalm 149:1-4)*

Sing unto the Lord a new song, and his praise from the end of the earth, ye that go down to the sea, and all that is therein; the isles, and the inhabitants thereof. . . . Let them give glory unto the Lord, and declare his praise in the islands. *(Isaiah 42:10,12)*

And after these things I heard a great voice of much people in heaven, saying, Alleluia: Salvation, and glory, and honor and power, unto the Lord our God. *(Revelation 19:1)*

Faith and Trust in God

Behold, happy is the man whom God correcteth; therefore despise not thou the chastening of the Almighty: for he maketh sore, and bindeth up: he woundeth, and his hands make whole. He shall deliver thee in six troubles: yea, in seven there shall no evil touch thee.

In famine he shall redeem thee from death: and in war from the power of the sword. Thou shalt be hid from the scourge of the tongue; neither shalt thou be afraid of destruction when it cometh. At destruction and famine thou shalt laugh; neither shalt thou be afraid of the beasts of the earth. For thou shalt be in league with the stones of the field; and the beasts of the field shall be at peace with thee. And thou shalt know that thy tabernacle shall be in peace; and thou shalt visit thy habitation, and shalt not sin. Thou shalt know also that thy seed shall be great, and thine offspring as the grass of the earth. Thou shalt come to thy grave in a full age, like a shock of corn cometh in his season. *(Job 5:17-26)*

The Lord is my rock, and my fortress, and my deliverer; my God, my strength, in whom I will trust; my buckler, and the horn of my salvation, and my high tower. *(Psalm 18:2)*

The Lord is my shepherd; I shall not want. He maketh me to lie down in green pastures: he leadeth me beside the still waters. He restoreth my soul: he leadeth me in the paths of righteousness for his name's sake. Yea, though I walk through the valley of the shadow of death, I will fear no evil; for thou art with me; thy rod and thy staff they comfort me.

Thou preparest a table before me in the presence of mine enemies: thou anointest my head with oil: my cup runneth over. Surely goodness and mercy shall follow me all the days of my life: and I will dwell in the house of the Lord for ever. *(Psalm 23:1-6)*

The Lord is my light and my salvation; whom shall I fear? the Lord is the strength of my life; of whom shall I be afraid? *(Psalm 27:1)*

What time I am afraid, I will trust in thee. In God I will praise his word, in God I have put my trust; I will not fear what flesh can do unto me. *(Psalm 56:3-4)*

Truly my soul waiteth upon God: from him cometh my salvation. He only is my rock, and my salvation; he is my defence; I shall not be greatly moved. . . . My soul, wait thou only upon God; for my expectation is from him. He only is my rock and my salvation: he is my defence; I shall not be moved. In God is my salvation and my glory: the rock of my strength, and my refuge, is in God. Trust in him at all times; ye people, pour out your heart before him; God is a refuge for us. *(Psalm 62:1,2,5-8)*

He that dwelleth in the secret place of the Most High, shall abide under the shadow of the Almighty. I will say of the Lord, He is my refuge and my fortress: my God: in him will I trust. Surely he shall deliver thee from the snare of the fowler, and from the noisome pestilence. He shall cover thee with his feathers, and under his wings shalt thou trust: his truth shall be thy shield and buckler. Thou shalt not be afraid for the terror by night; nor for the arrow that flieth by day; nor for the pestilence that walketh in darkness; nor for the destruction that wasteth at noonday. *(Psalm 91:1-6)*

Because thou hast made the Lord, which is my refuge, even the Most High, thy habitation; there shall no evil befall thee, neither shall any plague come nigh thy dwelling. For he shall give his angels charge over thee, to keep thee in all thy ways. *(Psalm 91:9-11)*

Behold, God is my salvation; I will trust, and not be afraid: for the Lord Jehovah is my strength and my song; he also is become my salvation. *(Isaiah 12:2)*

Although the fig tree shall not blossom, neither shall fruit be in the vines; the labor of the olive shall fail, and the fields shall yield no meat; the flock shall be cut off from the fold, and there shall be no herd in the stalls: yet I will rejoice in the Lord, I will joy in the God of my salvation. The Lord God is my strength, and he will make my feet like hinds' feet,

and he will make me to walk upon my high places.
(Habakkuk 3:17-19)

Confession and Forgiveness

If I shut up heaven that there be no rain, or if I
command the locusts to devour the land, or if I send
pestilence among my people; if my people, which are
called by my name, shall humble themselves, and
pray, and seek my face, and turn from their wicked
ways; then will I hear from heaven, and will forgive
their sin, and will heal their land. *(2 Chronicles
7:13-14)*

I fell upon my knees, and spread out my hands
unto the Lord my God, and said, O my God, I am
ashamed and blush to lift up my face to thee, my God:
for our iniquities are increased over our head, and our
trespass is grown up unto the heavens. *(Ezra 9:5-6)*

Let thine ear now be attentive, and thine eyes
open, that thou mayest hear the prayer of thy servant,
which I pray before thee now, day and night, for the
children of Israel thy servants, and confess the sins
of the children of Israel, which we have sinned
against thee: both I and my father's house have
sinned. We have dealt very corruptly against thee,
and have not kept the commandments, nor the statutes, nor the judgments, which thou commandedst

thy servant Moses. *(Nehemiah 1:6-7)*

For innumerable evils have compassed me about: my iniquities have taken hold upon me, so that I am not able to look up; they are more than the hairs of mine head: therefore my heart faileth me. Be pleased, O Lord, to deliver me: O Lord, make haste to help me. *(Psalm 40:12-13)*

Have mercy upon me, O God, according to thy lovingkindness: according unto the multitude of thy tender mercies blot out my transgressions. Wash me thoroughly from mine iniquity, and cleanse me from my sin. For I acknowledge my transgressions: and my sin is ever before me. Against thee, thee only, have I sinned, and done this evil in thy sight: that thou mightest be justified when thou speakest, and be clear when thou judgest. *(Psalm 51:1-4)*

For our transgressions are multiplied before thee, and our sins testify against us: for our transgressions are with us; and as for our iniquities, we know them; In transgressing and lying against the Lord, and departing away from our God, speaking oppression and revolt, conceiving and uttering from the heart words of falsehood. And judgment is turned away backward, and justice standeth afar off: for truth is fallen in the street, and equity cannot enter. Yea, truth faileth; and he that departeth from evil maketh himself a prey. *(Isaiah 59:12-15)*

We have sinned, and have committed iniquity, and have done wickedly, and have rebelled, even by departing from thy precepts and from thy judgments: Neither have we hearkened unto thy servants the prophets, which spake in thy name to our kings, our princes, and our fathers, and to all the people of the land. O Lord, righteousness belongeth unto thee. . . .

O Lord, to us belongeth confusion of face, to our kings, to our princes, and to our fathers, because we have sinned against thee. To the Lord our God belong mercies and forgivenesses, though we have rebelled against him. *(Daniel 9:5-6,8-9)*

For if ye forgive men their trespasses, your heavenly Father will also forgive you: but if ye forgive not men their trespasses, neither will your Father forgive your trespasses. *(Matthew 6:14-15)*

And when they were come to the place, which is called Calvary, there they crucified him, and the malefactors, one on the right hand, and the other on the left. Then said Jesus, Father, forgive them; for they know not what they do. *(Luke 23:33-34a)*

And they stoned Stephen, calling upon God, and saying, Lord Jesus, receive my spirit. And he kneeled down, and cried with a loud voice, Lord, lay not this sin to their charge. And when he had said this, he fell asleep. *(Acts 7:59-60)*

For all have sinned, and come short of the glory of God. *(Romans 3:23)*

Not by works of righteousness which we have done, but according to his mercy he saved us, by the washing of regeneration, and renewing of the Holy Ghost. *(Titus 3:5)*

Let us therefore come boldly unto the throne of grace that we may obtain mercy, and find grace to help in time of need. *(Hebrews 4:16)*

Prayer and Supplication

But if from thence thou shalt seek the Lord thy God, thou shalt find him, if thou seek him with all thy heart and with all thy soul. When thou art in tribulation, and all these things are come upon thee, even in the latter days, if thou turn to the Lord thy God, and shalt be obedient unto his voice; (For the Lord thy God is a merciful God;) he will not forsake thee, neither destroy thee, nor forget the covenant of thy fathers which he sware unto them. *(Deuteronomy 4:29-31)*

Yet have thou respect unto the prayer of thy servant, and to his supplication, O Lord my God, to hearken unto the cry and to the prayer, which thy servant prayeth before thee to day: That thine eyes may be open toward this house night and day, even toward the place of which thou hast said, My name shall be there: that thou mayest hearken unto the prayer which thy servant shall make toward this place. *(1 Kings 8:28-29)*

The Lord hath heard my supplication; the Lord will receive my prayer. *(Psalm 6:9)*

Show me thy ways, O Lord; teach me thy paths. Lead me in thy truth, and teach me: for thou art the God of my salvation; on thee do I wait all the day. Remember, O Lord, thy tender mercies and thy lovingkindnesses; for they have been ever of old. Remember not the sins of my youth, nor my transgressions: according to thy mercy remember thou me for thy goodness' sake, O Lord. *(Psalm 25:4-7)*

And call upon me in the day of trouble: I will deliver thee, and thou shalt glorify me. *(Psalm 50:15)*

Have mercy upon me, O God, according to thy lovingkindness: according unto the multitude of thy tender mercies blot out my transgressions. Wash me thoroughly from mine iniquity, and cleanse me from my sin. . . . Hide thy face from my sins, and blot out all my iniquities. Create in me a clean heart, O God; and renew a right spirit within me. Cast me not away from thy presence; and take not thy holy spirit from me. Restore unto me the joy of thy salvation; and uphold me with thy free spirit. Then will I teach transgressors thy ways; and sinners shall be converted unto thee. *(Psalm 51:1-2,9-13)*

Hear me, O Lord; for thy lovingkindness is good: turn unto me according to the multitude of thy tender mercies. And hide not thy face from thy servant; for I am in trouble: hear me speedily. Draw nigh unto my soul and redeem it: deliver me because of mine enemies. *(Psalm 69:16-18)*

O Lord God of my salvation, I have cried day and night before thee: Let my prayer come before thee: incline thine ear unto my cry. *(Psalm 88:1-2)*

Teach me, O Lord, the way of thy statutes; and I shall keep it unto the end. Give me understanding, and I shall keep thy law; yea, I shall observe it with my whole heart. Make me to go in the path of thy commandments; for therein do I delight. Incline my heart unto thy testimonies, and not to covetousness. Turn away mine eyes from beholding vanity; and quicken thou me in thy way. Establish thy word unto thy servant, who is devoted to thy fear. Turn away my reproach which I fear: for thy judgments are good. Behold, I have longed after thy precepts: quicken me in thy righteousness. *(Psalm 119:33-40)*

Out of the depths have I cried unto thee, O Lord.

Lord, hear my voice: let thine ears be attentive to the
voice of my supplications. If thou, Lord, shouldest
mark iniquities, O Lord, who shall stand? But there
is forgiveness with thee, that thou mayest be feared.

I wait for the Lord, my soul doth wait, and in his
word do I hope. My soul waiteth for the Lord more
than they that watch for the morning: I say, more than
they that watch for the morning. Let Israel hope in
the Lord, for with the Lord there is mercy, and with
him is plenteous redemption. And he shall redeem
Israel from all his iniquities. *(Psalm 130:1-8)*

Hear my prayer, O Lord, give ear to my supplications: in thy faithfulness answer me, and in thy
righteousness. . . . Hear me speedily, O Lord; my
spirit faileth; hide not thy face from me, lest I be like
unto them that go down into the pit. Cause me to hear
thy lovingkindness in the morning; for in thee do I
trust; cause me to know the way wherein I should
walk; for I lift up my soul unto thee. (Psalm 143:1,7-8)

And it shall come to pass, that before they call, I
will answer; and while they are yet speaking, I will
hear. *(Isaiah 65:24)*

And when thou prayest, thou shalt not be as the
hypocrites are: for they love to pray standing in the
synagogues and in the corners of the streets, that they
may be seen of men. Verily I say unto you, They have

their reward. But thou, when thou prayest, enter into thy closet, and when thou hast shut thy door, pray to thy Father which is in secret; and thy Father which seeth in secret shall reward thee openly. But when ye pray, use not vain repetitions, as the heathen do: for they think that they shall be heard for their much speaking. Be not ye therefore like unto them: for your Father knoweth what things ye have need of, before ye ask him. After this manner therefore pray ye: Our Father which art in heaven, Hallowed be thy name. Thy kingdom come. Thy will be done in earth as it is in heaven. Give us this day our daily bread. And forgive us our debts, as we forgive our debtors. And lead us not into temptation, but deliver us from evil. For thine is the kingdom, and the power, and the glory, for ever. Amen. *(Matthew 6:5-13)*

And I say unto you, Ask, and it shall be given you; seek, and ye shall find; knock, and it shall be opened unto you. For every one that asketh receiveth; and he that seeketh findeth; and to him that knocketh it shall be opened. If a son shall ask bread of any of you that is a father, will he give him a stone? or if he ask a fish, will he for a fish give him a serpent? Or if he shall ask an egg, will he offer him a scorpion? If ye then, being evil, know how to give good gifts unto your children: how much more shall your heavenly Father give the Holy Spirit to them that ask him? *(Luke 11:9-13)*

And he spake this parable unto certain which trusted in themselves that they were righteous, and despised others: Two men went up into the temple to pray; the one a Pharisee and the other a publican. The Pharisee stood and prayed thus with himself, God, I thank thee, that I am not as other men are, extortioners, unjust, adulterers, or even as this publican. I fast twice in the week, I give tithes of all that I possess. And the publican, standing afar off, would not lift up so much as his eyes unto heaven, but smote upon his breast, saying, God be merciful to me a sinner. I tell you, this man went down to his house justified rather than the other: for every one that exalteth himself shall be abased; and he that humbleth himself shall be exalted. *(Luke 18:9-14)*

Verily, verily, I say unto you, Whatsoever ye shall ask the Father in my name, he will give it to you. Hitherto have ye asked nothing in my name: ask, and ye shall receive, that your joy may be full. *(John 16:23-24)*

And this is the confidence that we have in him, that if we ask any thing according to his will, he heareth us: And if we know that he hear us, whatsoever we ask, we know that we have the petitions that we desired of him. *(1 John 5:14-15)*

Christian Love

Ye have heard that it hath been said, Thou shalt love thy neighbor, and hate thine enemy. But I say unto you, Love your enemies, bless them that curse you, do good to them that hate you, and pray for them which despitefully use you, and persecute you; that you may be the children of your Father which is in heaven: for he maketh his sun to rise on the evil and on the good, and sendeth rain on the just and on the unjust.

For if you love them which love you, what reward have ye? do not even the publicans the same? And if ye salute your brethren only, what do ye more than others? do not even the publicans so? Be ye therefore perfect, even as your Father which is in heaven is perfect. *(Matthew 5:43-48)*

Then one of them, which was a lawyer, asked him a question, tempting him, and saying, Master, which is the great commandment in the law?

Jesus said unto him, Thou shalt love the Lord thy God with all thy heart, and with all thy soul, and with all thy mind. This is the first and great commandment. And the second is like unto it, Thou shalt love thy neighbor as thyself. On these two commandments hang all the law and the prophets.

But I say unto you which hear, Love your enemies,

do good to them which hate you. Bless them that curse you, and pray for them which despitefully use you. And unto him that smiteth thee on the one cheek offer also the other; and him that taketh away thy cloak forbid not to take thy coat also. Give to every man that asketh of thee, and of him that taketh away thy goods ask them not again. And as ye would that men should do to you, do ye also to them likewise. *(Luke 6:27-31)*

For God so loved the world, that he gave his only begotten Son, that whosoever believeth in him should not perish, but have everlasting life. *(John 3:16)*

A new commandment I give unto you, that ye love one another; as I have loved you, that ye also love one another. By this shall all men know that ye are my disciples, if ye have love one to another. *(John 13:34-35)*

This is my commandment, That ye love one another, as I have loved you. Greater love hath no man than this, that a man lay down his life for his friends. *(John 15:12-13)*

Who shall separate us from the love of Christ? shall tribulation, or distress, or persecution, or famine, or nakedness, or peril, or sword? As it is written, For thy sake we are killed all the day long; we are accounted as sheep for the slaughter. Nay, in all these things we are more than conquerors through him that loved us. For I am persuaded, that neither death, nor life, nor angels, nor principalities, nor powers, nor things present, nor things to come, nor height, nor depth, nor any other creature, shall be able to separate us from the love of God, which is in Christ Jesus, our Lord. *(Romans 8:35-39)*

Though I speak with the tongues of men and of angels, and have not love, I am become as sounding brass, or a tinkling cymbal. And though I have the gift of prophecy and understand all mysteries and all knowledge; and though I have all faith, so that I could remove mountains, and have not love, I am nothing. And though I bestow all my goods to feed the poor, and though I give my body to be burned, and have not love, it profiteth me nothing.

Love suffereth long, and is kind; love envieth not, love vaunteth not itself, is not puffed up, doth not behave itself unseemly, seeketh not her own, is not easily provoked, thinketh no evil; rejoiceth not in iniquity, but rejoiceth in the truth; beareth all things, believeth all things, hopeth all things, endureth all things.

Love never faileth, but whether there be prophecies, they shall fail; whether there be tongues, they shall cease; whether there be knowledge, it shall vanish away. And now abideth faith, hope, love, these three; but the greatest of these is love. *(1 Corinthians 13:1-8,13, substituting the word love for charity)*

But the fruit of the Spirit is love, joy, peace, longsuffering, gentleness, goodness, faith, meekness, temperance: against such there is no law. *(Galatians 5:22-23)*

Brethren, if a man be overtaken in a fault, ye which are spiritual restore such a one in the spirit of meekness; considering thyself, lest thou also be tempted. Bear ye one another's burdens, and so fulfill the law of Christ. *(Galatians 6:1-2)*

Fulfil ye my joy, that ye be like-minded, having the same love, being of one accord, of one mind. Let nothing be done through strife or vainglory; but in lowliness of mind let each esteem other better than themselves. Look not every man on his own things, but every man also on the things of others. Let this mind be in you, which was also in Christ Jesus. *(Philippians 2:2-5)*

For this is the message that ye heard from the beginning, that we should love one another. *(1 John 3:11)*

Beloved, let us love one another, for love is of God; and every one that loveth is born of God, and knoweth God. He that loveth not knoweth not God, for God is love. In this was manifested the love of God toward us, because that God sent his only begotten Son into the world, that we might live through him. Herein is love, not that we loved God, but that he loved us, and sent his Son to be the propitiation for our sins. Beloved, if God so loved us, we ought also to love one another. *(1 John 4:7-11)*

And we have known and believed the love that God hath to us. God is love, and he that dwelleth in love dwelleth in God, and God in him. Herein is our love made perfect that we may have boldness in the day of judgment: because as he is, so are we in this world. There is no fear in love; but perfect love casteth out fear: because fear hath torment. He that feareth is not made perfect in love. We love him, because he first loved us. If a man say, I love God, and hateth his brother, he is a liar: for he that loveth not his brother whom he hath seen, how can he love God whom he hath not seen? And this commandment have we from him, That he who loveth God love his brother also. *(1 John 4:16-21)*

Spreading the Word

All the ends of the world shall remember and turn unto the Lord: and all the kindreds of the nations shall worship before thee. *(Psalm 22:27)*

Declare his glory among the heathen, his wonders among all people. For the Lord is great, and greatly to be praised: he is to be feared above all gods. For all the gods of the nations are idols; but the Lord made the heavens. *(Psalm 96:3-5)*

How beautiful upon the mountains are the feet of him that bringeth good tidings, that publisheth peace; that bringeth good tidings of good, that publisheth salvation; that saith unto Zion, Thy God reigneth! *(Isaiah 52:7)*

And Jesus, walking by the sea of Galilee, saw two brethren, Simon called Peter, and Andrew his brother, casting a net into the sea: for they were fishers. And he saith unto them, Follow me, and I will make you fishers of men. And they straightway left their nets, and followed him. *(Matthew 4:18-20)*

And this gospel of the kingdom shall be preached in all the world for a witness unto all nations; and then shall the end come. *(Matthew 24:14)*

And Jesus came and spake unto them, saying, All power is given unto me in heaven and in earth. Go ye therefore, and teach all nations, baptizing them in the name of the Father, and of the Son, and of the Holy Ghost: teaching them to observe all things whatsoever I have commanded you: and, lo, I am with you alway, even unto the end of the world. Amen. *(Matthew 28:18-20)*

And the gospel must first be published among all nations. *(Mark 13:10)*

Go ye into all the world, and preach the gospel to every creature. He that believeth, and is baptized, shall be saved; but he that believeth not shall be damned. *(Mark 16:15-16)*

After these things the Lord appointed other seventy also, and sent them two and two before his face into every city and place, whither he himself would come. Therefore said he unto them, The harvest truly is great, but the laborers are few: pray ye therefore the Lord of the harvest, that he would send forth laborers into his harvest. *(Luke 10:1-2)*

I am the good shepherd, and know my sheep, and am known of mine. As the Father knoweth me, even so know I the Father: and I lay down my life for the sheep. And other sheep I have, which are not of this fold: them also I must bring, and they shall hear my voice; and there shall be one fold, and one shepherd. *(John 10:14-16)*

Then said Jesus to them again, Peace be unto you: as my Father hath sent me, even so send I you. *(John 20:21)*

When they therefore were come together, they asked of him, saying, Lord, wilt thou at this time restore again the kingdom to Israel? And he said unto them, It is not for you to know the times or the seasons, which the Father hath put in his own power. But ye shall receive power, after that the Holy Ghost is come upon you: and ye shall be witnesses unto me both in Jerusalem, and in all Judea, and in Samaria, and unto the uttermost part of the earth. *(Acts 1:6-8)*

But Peter, standing up with the eleven, lifted up his voice, and said unto them, Ye men of Judea, and all ye that dwell at Jerusalem, be this known unto you, and hearken to my words: . . . This is that which was spoken by the prophet Joel; And it shall come to pass in the last days, saith God, I will pour out of my Spirit upon all flesh: and your sons and daughters shall prophesy, and your young men shall see visions, and your old men shall dream dreams: and on my servants and on my handmaidens I will pour out in those days of my Spirit; and they shall prophesy: . . . And it shall come to pass, that whosoever shall call on the name of the Lord shall be saved. *(Acts 2:14,16-18,21)*

And a vision appeared to Paul in the night; There stood a man of Macedonia, and prayed him, saying, Come over into Macedonia, and help us. And after he had seen the vision, immediately we endeavored to go into Macedonia, assuredly gathering that the Lord had called us for to preach the gospel unto them. *(Acts 16:9-10)*

Salvation

Let Israel hope in the Lord: for with the Lord there is mercy, and with him is plenteous redemption. *(Psalm 130:7)*

He that covereth his sins shall not prosper; but whoso confesseth and forsaketh them shall have mercy. *(Proverbs 28:13)*

Come now, and let us reason together, saith the Lord; though your sins be as scarlet, they shall be as white as snow; though they be red like crimson, they shall be as wool. *(Isaiah 1:18)*

Look unto me, and be ye saved, all the ends of the earth; for I am God, and there is none else. *(Isaiah 45:22)*

Come unto me, all ye that labor and are heavy laden, and I will give you rest. Take my yoke upon you, and learn of me; for I am meek and lowly in heart; and ye shall find rest unto your souls. *(Matthew 11:28-29)*

For God sent not his Son into the world to condemn the world; but that the world through him might be saved. *(John 3:17)*

He that believeth on the Son hath everlasting life. *(John 3:36)*

Verily, verily, I say unto you, He that believeth on me hath everlasting life. *(John 6:47)*

And at midnight Paul and Silas prayed, and sang praises unto God: and the prisoners heard them. And suddenly there was a great earthquake, so that the foundations of the prison were shaken: and immediately all the doors were opened, and every one's bands were loosed. And the keeper of the prison awaking out of his sleep, and seeing the prison doors open, he drew out his sword, and would have killed himself, supposing that the prisoners had been fled. But Paul cried with a loud voice, saying, Do thyself no harm; for we are all here.

Then he called for a light, and sprang in, and came trembling, and fell down before Paul and Silas, and brought them out, and said, Sirs, what must I do to be saved? And they said, Believe on the Lord Jesus Christ, and thou shalt be saved, and thy house. And they spake unto him the word of the Lord, and to all that were in his house. And he took them the same hour of the night, and washed their stripes; and was baptized, he and all his, straightway. And when he had brought them into his house, he set meat before them, and rejoiced, believing in God with all his house. *(Acts 16:25-34)*

If thou shalt confess with thy mouth the Lord Jesus, and shalt believe in thine heart that God hath raised him from the dead, thou shalt be saved. *(Romans 10:9)*

For by grace are ye saved through faith; and that not of yourselves; it is the gift of God: not of works, lest any man should boast. *(Ephesians 2:8-9)*

Not by works of righteousness which we have done, but according to his mercy he saved us, by the washing of regeneration, and renewing of the Holy Ghost. *(Titus 3:5)*

Invitation to Discipleship

Ho, every one that thirsteth, come ye to the waters, and he that hath no money; come ye, buy, and eat; yea, come, buy wine and milk without money and without price. Wherefore do ye spend money for that which is not bread? and your labor for that which satisfieth not? hearken diligently unto me, and eat ye that which is good, and let your soul delight itself in fatness. Incline your ear, and come unto me: hear, and your soul shall live; and I will make an everlasting covenant with you, even the sure mercies of David. *(Isaiah 55:1-3)*

Seek ye the Lord while he may be found, call ye
upon him while he is near: Let the wicked forsake his
way, and the unrighteous man his thoughts: and let
him return unto the Lord, and he will have mercy
upon him, and to our God, for he will abundantly
pardon. For my thoughts are not your thoughts, neither are your ways my ways, saith the Lord. For as
the heavens are higher than the earth, so are my ways
higher than your ways, and my thoughts than your
thoughts. *(Isaiah 55:6-9)*

Ask, and it shall be given you; seek, and ye shall
find; knock, and it shall be opened unto you: For
every one that asketh receiveth; and he that seeketh
findeth; and to him that knocketh it shall be opened.
(Matthew 7:7-8)

They that be whole need not a physician, but they
that are sick. But go ye and learn what that meaneth,
I will have mercy, and not sacrifice: for I am not come
to call the righteous, but sinners to repentance. *(Matthew 9:12-13)*

Come unto me, all ye that labor and are heavy laden,
and I will give you rest. Take my yoke upon you, and
learn of me; for I am meek and lowly in heart: and
ye shall find rest unto your souls. For my yoke is
easy, and my burden is light. *(Matthew 11:28-30)*

And Jesus said unto them, I am the bread of life:

he that cometh to me shall never hunger; and he that believeth on me shall never thirst. But I said unto you, That ye also have seen me, and believe not. All that the Father giveth me shall come to me; and him that cometh to me I will in no wise cast out. For I came down from heaven, not to do mine own will, but the will of him that sent me. And this is the Father's will which hath sent me, that of all which he hath given me I should lose nothing, but should raise it up again at the last day. And this is the will of him that sent me, that every one which seeth the Son, and believeth on him, may have everlasting life: and I will raise him up at the last day. *(John 6:35-40)*

If any man thirst, let him come unto me, and drink. He that believeth on me, as the scripture hath said, out of his belly shall flow rivers of living water. *(John 7:37-38)*

And the Spirit and the bride say, Come. And let him that heareth say, Come. And let him that is athirst come. And whosoever will, let him take the water of life freely. *(Revelation 22:17)*

Good Works

Thou shalt have no other gods before me.

Thou shalt not make unto thee any graven image, or any likeness of any thing that is in heaven above, or that is in the earth beneath, or that is in the water under the earth. Thou shalt not bow down thyself to them, nor serve them: for I the Lord thy God am a jealous God, visiting the iniquity of the fathers upon the children unto the third and fourth generation of them that hate me; and showing mercy unto thousands of them that love me, and keep my commandments.

Thou shalt not take the name of the Lord thy God in vain; for the Lord will not hold him guiltless that taketh his name in vain.

Remember the sabbath day, to keep it holy. Six days shalt thou labor, and do all thy work: but the seventh day is the sabbath of the Lord thy God: in it thou shalt not do any work, thou, nor thy son, nor thy daughter, thy manservant, nor thy maidservant, nor thy cattle, nor thy stranger that is within thy gates. For in six days the Lord made heaven and earth, the sea, and all in them is, and rested the seventh day: wherefore the Lord blessed the sabbath day, and hallowed it.

Honor thy father and thy mother: that thy days may be long upon the land which the Lord thy God giveth thee.

Thou shalt not kill.

Thou shalt not commit adultery.

Thou shalt not steal.

Thou shalt not bear false witness against thy neighbor.

Thou shalt not covet thy neighbor's house, thou shalt not covet thy neighbor's wife, nor his manservant, nor his maidservant, nor his ox, nor his ass, nor any thing that is thy neighbor's. *(Exodus 20:3-17)*

To do justice and judgment is more acceptable to the Lord than sacrifice. *(Proverbs 21:3)*

Seek good, and not evil, that ye may live: and so the Lord, the God of hosts, shall be with you, as ye have spoken. *(Amos 5:14)*

He hath showed thee, O man, what is good; and what doth the Lord require of thee, but to do justly, and to love mercy, and to walk humbly with thy God? *(Micah 6:8)*

But seek ye first the kingdom of God, and his righteousness; and all these things shall be added unto you. *(Matthew 6:33)*

Then shall the King say unto them on his right hand, Come, ye blessed of my Father, inherit the kingdom prepared for you from the foundation of the world: For I was an hungered, and ye gave me meat: I was thirsty, and ye gave me drink: I was a stranger, and ye took me in: Naked and ye clothed me: I was sick, and ye visited me: I was in prison, and ye came unto me. Then shall the righteous answer him, saying, Lord, when saw we thee an hungered, and fed thee? or thirsty, and gave thee drink? When saw we thee a stranger, and took thee in? or naked, and clothed thee? Or when saw we thee sick, or in prison, and came unto thee? And the King shall answer and say unto them, Verily I say unto you, Inasmuch as ye have done it unto one of the least of these my brethren, ye have done it unto me. *(Matthew 25:34-40)*

And Jesus answering said, A certain man went down from Jerusalem to Jericho, and fell among thieves, which stripped him of his raiment, and wounded him, and departed, leaving him half dead. And by chance there came down a certain priest that way: and when he saw him, he passed by on the other side. And likewise a Levite, when he was at the place, came and looked on him, and passed by on the other side. But a certain Samaritan, as he journeyed, came where he was: and when he saw him, he had compassion on him, and went to him, and bound up his wounds, pouring in oil and wine, and set him on his own beast, and brought him to an inn, and took care of him. And on the morrow when he departed, he took out two pence, and gave them to the host, and said unto him, Take care of him; and whatsoever thou spendest more, when I come again, I will repay thee. Which now of these three, thinkest thou, was neighbor unto him that fell among the thieves? *(Luke 10:30-36)*

Sell that ye have, and give alms; provide yourselves bags which wax not old, a treasure in the heavens that faileth not, where no thief approacheth, neither moth corrupteth. For where your treasure is, there will your heart be also. *(Luke 12:33-34)*

Finally, brethren, whatsoever things are true, whatsoever things are honest, whatsoever things are just, whatsoever things are pure, whatsoever things are lovely, whatsoever things are of good report; if there be any virtue, and if there be any praise, think on these things. *(Philippians 4:8)*

What doth it profit, my brethren, though a man say he hath faith, and have not works? can faith save him? If a brother or sister be naked, and destitute of daily food, and one of you say unto them, Depart in peace, be ye warmed and filled; notwithstanding ye give him not these things which are needful to the body; what doth it profit? Even so faith, if it hath not works, is dead, being alone. Yea, a man may say, Thou hast faith, and I have works: show me thy faith without thy works, and I will show thee my faith by my works. For as the body without the spirit is dead, so faith without works is dead also. *(James 2:14-18,26)*

And I heard a voice from heaven saying unto me, Write, Blessed are the dead which die in the Lord from henceforth. Yea, saith the Spirit, that they may rest from their labors; and their works do follow them. *(Revelation 14:13)*

Stewardship

And Jacob vowed a vow, saying, If God will be with me, and will keep me in this way that I go, and will give me bread to eat, and raiment to put on, so that I come again to my father's house in peace; then shall the Lord be my God. And this stone, which I have set for a pillar, shall be God's house: and of all that thou shalt give me I will surely give the tenth unto thee. *(Genesis 28:20-22)*

The children of Israel brought a willing offering unto the Lord, every man and woman, whose heart made them willing to bring for all manner of work, which the Lord had commanded to be made by the hand of Moses. *(Exodus 35:29)*

And all the tithe of the land, whether of the seed of the land, or of the fruit of the tree, is the Lord's: it is holy unto the Lord. *(Leviticus 27:30)*

Every man shall give as he is able, according to the blessing of the Lord thy God which he hath given thee. *(Deuteronomy 16:17)*

Now therefore, our God, we thank thee, and praise

thy glorious name. But who am I, and what is my people, that we should be able to offer so willingly after this sort? for all things come of thee, and of thine own have we given thee. *(1 Chronicles 29:13-14)*

Give unto the Lord the glory due unto his name: bring an offering, and come into his courts. *(Psalm 96:8)*

Honor the Lord with thy substance, and with the firstfruits of all thine increase. *(Proverbs 3:9)*

For the kingdom of heaven is as a man traveling into a far country, who called his own servants, and delivered unto them his goods. And unto one he gave five talents, to another two, and to another one; to every man according to his several ability, and straightway took his journey. Then he that had received the five talents went and traded with the same, and made them other five talents. And likewise he that had received two, he also gained other two. But he that had received one went and digged in the earth, and hid his lord's money.

After a long time the lord of those servants cometh, and reckoneth with them. And so he that had received five talents came and brought other five talents, saying, Lord, thou deliveredst unto me five talents: behold, I have gained beside them five talents more. His lord said unto him, Well done, thou good and faithful servant: thou hast been faithful over a few things, I will make thee ruler over many things: enter thou into the joy of thy lord.

He also that had received two talents came and said, Lord, thou deliveredst unto me two talents: behold, I have gained two other talents beside them. His lord said unto him, Well done, good and faithful servant; thou hast been faithful over a few things, I will make thee ruler over many things: enter thou into the joy of thy lord.

Then he which had received the one talent came and said, Lord, I knew thee that thou art an hard man, reaping where thou hast not sown, and gathering where thou hast not strawed. And I was afraid, and went and hid thy talent in the earth: lo, there thou hast that is thine. His lord answered and said unto him, Thou wicked and slothful servant, thou knewest that I reap where I sowed not, and gather where I have not strawed. Thou oughtest therefore to have put my money to the exchangers, and then at my coming I should have received my own with usury. Take therefore the talent from him, and give it unto him which hath ten talents. For unto every one that hath shall be given, and he shall have abundance, but from him that hath not shall be taken away even that which he hath. (Matthew 25:14-29)

And Jesus sat over against the treasury, and beheld how the people cast money into the treasury: and many that were rich cast in much. And there came a certain poor widow, and she threw in two mites, which make a farthing. And he called unto him his disciples, and saith unto them, Verily I say unto you, That this poor widow hath cast more in, than all they which have cast into the treasury: for all they did cast in of their abundance; but she of her want did cast in all that she had, even all her living. *(Mark 12:41-44)*

Unto whomsoever much is given, of him shall be much required: and to whom men have committed much, of him they will ask the more. *(Luke 12:48b)*

I have showed you all things, how that so laboring ye ought to support the weak, and to remember the words of the Lord Jesus, how he said, It is more blessed to give than to receive. *(Acts 20:35)*

I beseech you therefore, brethren, by the mercies of God, that ye present your bodies a living sacrifice, holy, acceptable unto God, which is your reasonable service. And be not conformed to this world: but be ye transformed by the renewing of your mind, that ye may prove what is that good, and acceptable, and perfect, will of God. *(Romans 12:1-2)*

Upon the first day of the week let every one of

you lay by him in store, as God hath prospered him. *(1 Corinthians 16:2a)*

Every man according as he purposeth in his heart, so let him give; not grudgingly, or of necessity: for God loveth a cheerful giver. *(2 Corinthians 9:7)*

As every man hath received the gift, even so minister the same one to another, as good stewards of the manifold grace of God. *(1 Peter 4:10)*

The Christian Ministry

How beautiful upon the mountains are the feet of him that bringeth good tidings, that publisheth peace; that bringeth good tidings of good, that publisheth salvation; that saith unto Zion, Thy God reigneth! Thy watchmen shall lift up the voice; with the voice together shall they sing: for they shall see eye to eye, when the Lord shall bring again Zion. *(Isaiah 52:7-8)*

And Jesus went about all the cities and villages, teaching in their synagogues, and preaching the gospel of the kingdom, and healing every sickness and every disease among the people. But when he saw the multitudes, he was moved with compassion on them, because they fainted, and were scattered abroad, as sheep having no shepherd. Then saith he unto his disciples, The harvest truly is plenteous, but the laborers are few; Pray ye therefore the Lord of the harvest, that he will send forth laborers into his harvest. *(Matthew 9:35-38)*

He that receiveth you, receiveth me, and he that receiveth me receiveth him that sent me. He that receiveth a prophet in the name of a prophet shall receive a prophet's reward; and he that receiveth a righteous man in the name of a righteous man shall receive a righteous man's reward. And whosoever shall give to drink unto one of these little ones a cup of cold water only in the name of the disciple, verily, I say unto you, he shall in no wise lose his reward. *(Matthew 10:40-42)*

After these things, the Lord appointed other seventy also, and sent them two and two before his face, into every city and place, whither he himself would come. Therefore said he unto them, The harvest truly is great, but the laborers are few: pray ye therefore the Lord of the harvest, that he would send forth laborers into his harvest. Go your ways: behold, I send you forth as lambs among wolves. *(Luke 10:1-3)*

Then said Jesus to them again, Peace be unto you: as my Father hath sent me, even so send I you. And when he had said this, he breathed on them, and saith unto them, Receive ye the Holy Spirit. *(John 20:21-22)*

Jesus saith to Simon Peter, Simon, son of Jonas, lovest thou me more than these? He saith unto him,

Yea, Lord; thou knowest that I love thee. He saith unto him, Feed my lambs. He saith to him again the second time, Simon, son of Jonas, lovest thou me? He saith unto him, Yea, Lord, thou knowest that I love thee. He saith unto him, Feed my sheep. He saith unto him the third time, Simon, son of Jonas, lovest thou me? Peter was grieved because he said unto him the third time, Lovest thou me? And he said unto him, Lord, thou knowest all things; thou knowest that I love thee. Jesus saith unto him, Feed my sheep. *(John 21:15-17)*

How then shall they call on him in whom they have not believed? and how shall they believe in him of whom they have not heard? and how shall they hear without a preacher? And how shall they preach except they be sent? As it is written, How beautiful are the feet of them that preach the gospel of peace, and bring glad tidings of good things! *(Romans 10:14-15)*

Therefore, seeing we have this ministry, as we have received mercy, we faint not; but have renounced the hidden things of dishonesty, not walking in craftiness, nor handling the word of God deceitfully; but by manifestation of the truth commending ourselves to every man's conscience in the sight of God. . . . For we preach not ourselves, but Christ Jesus the Lord; and ourselves your servants for Jesus' sake. *(2 Corinthians 4:1-2,5)*

Giving no offence in any thing, that the ministry be not blamed: but in all things approving ourselves as the ministers of God. *(2 Corinthians 6:3-4a)*

I [Paul] was made a minister, according to the gift of the grace of God given unto me by the effectual working of his power. Unto me, who am less than the least of all saints, is this grace given, that I should preach among the Gentiles the unsearchable riches of Christ; and to make all men see what is the fellowship of the mystery, which from the beginning of the world hath been hid in God, who created all things by Jesus Christ: to the intent that now unto the principalities and powers in heavenly places might be known by the church the manifold wisdom of God, according to the eternal purpose which he purposed in Christ Jesus our Lord. *(Ephesians 3:7-11)*

And he gave some, apostles; and some, prophets; and some, evangelists; and some, pastors and teachers; for the perfecting of the saints, for the work of the ministry, for the edifying of the body of Christ: till we all come in the unity of the faith, and of the knowledge of the Son of God, unto a perfect man, unto the measure of the stature of the fulness of Christ. *(Ephesians 4:11-13)*

If a man desire the office of a bishop, he desireth a good work. A bishop must then be blameless, the husband of one wife, vigilant, sober, of good behavior, given to hospitality, apt to teach; not given to wine, no striker, not greedy of filthy lucre; but patient, not a brawler, not covetous. *(1 Timothy 3:1b-3)*

Neglect not the gift that is in thee, which was given thee by prophecy, with the laying on of the hands of the presbytery. Meditate upon these things; give thyself wholly to them; that they profiting may appear to all. Take heed unto thyself, and unto the doctrine; continue in them: for in doing this thou shalt both save thyself, and them that hear thee. *(1 Timothy 4:14-16)*

Fight the good fight of faith, lay hold on eternal life, whereunto thou art also called, and hast professed a good profession before many witnesses. . . . Charge them that are rich in this world, that they be not high-minded, nor trust in uncertain riches, but in the living God, who giveth us richly all things to enjoy: that they do good, that they be rich in good works, ready to distribute, willing to communicate; laying up in store for themselves a good foundation against the time to come, that they may lay hold on eternal life. *(1 Timothy 6:12,17-19)*

Thou therefore, my son, be strong in the grace that is in Christ Jesus. And the things that thou hast heard of me among many witnesses, the same commit thou to faithful men, who shall be able to teach others also. Thou, therefore, endure hardness, as a good soldier of Jesus Christ. *(2 Timothy 2:1-3)*

Study to shew thyself approved unto God, a workman that needeth not to be ashamed, rightly dividing the word of truth. But shun profane and vain babblings; for they will increase unto more ungodliness. *(2 Timothy 2:15-16)*

I charge thee therefore before God, and the Lord Jesus Christ, who shall judge the quick and the dead at his appearing and his kingdom; Preach the word; be instant in season, out of season; reprove, rebuke, exhort with all longsuffering and doctrine. For the time will come when they will not endure sound doctrine; but after their own lusts shall they heap to themselves teachers, having itching ears; and they shall turn away their ears from the truth, and shall be turned unto fables. But watch thou in all things, endure affliction, do the work of an evangelist, make full proof of thy ministry. *(2 Timothy 4:1-5)*

But speak thou the things which become sound doctrine. . . . In all things showing thyself a pattern of good works: in doctrine showing uncorruptness, gravity, sincerity, sound speech, that cannot be condemned; that he that is of the contrary part may be ashamed, having no evil thing to say of you. . . . For the grace of God that bringeth salvation hath appeared to all men, teaching us that, denying ungodliness and worldly lusts, we should live soberly, righteously, and godly, in this present world; looking for that blessed hope, and the glorious appearing of the great God and our Saviour Jesus Christ; who gave himself for us, that he might redeem us from all iniquity, and purify unto himself a peculiar people, zealous of good works. These things speak, and exhort, and rebuke with all authority. Let no man despise thee. *(Titus 2:1,7-8,11-15)*

As every man hath received the gift, even so minister the same one to another, as good stewards of the manifold grace of God. If any man speak, let him speak as the oracles of God; if any man minister, let him do it as of the ability which God giveth: that God in all things may be glorified through Jesus Christ, to whom be praise and dominion for ever and ever. *(1 Peter 4:10-11)*

Feed the flock of God which is among you, taking the oversight thereof, not by constraint, but willingly: not for filthy lucre, but of a ready mind; neither as being lords over God's heritage, but being ensamples to the flock. And when the chief Shepherd shall appear, ye shall receive a crown of glory that fadeth not away. *(1 Peter 5:2-4)*

Laity

And Moses said unto him, Enviest thou for my sake? would God that all the Lord's people were prophets, and that the Lord would put his spirit upon them! *(Numbers 11:29)*

And in those days, when the number of the disciples was multiplied, there arose a murmuring of the Grecians against the Hebrews, because their widows were neglected in the daily ministration. Then the twelve called the multitude of the disciples unto them, and said, It is not reason that we should leave the word of God, and serve tables. Wherefore, brethren, look ye out among you seven men of honest report, full of the Holy Ghost and wisdom, whom we may appoint over this business. But we will give ourselves continually to prayer, and to the ministry of the word. And the saying pleased the whole multitude: and they chose Stephen, a man full of faith and of the Holy Ghost; and Philip, and Prochorus, and Nicanor, and Timon, and Parmenas, and Nicolas a proselyte of Antioch: whom they set before the apostles: and when they had prayed, they laid their hands on them. And the word of God increased; and the number of the disciples multiplied in Jerusalem greatly; and a great company of the priests were obedient to the faith. *(Acts 6:1-7)*

And a certain woman named Lydia, a seller of purple, of the city of Thyatira, which worshiped God, heard us: whose heart the Lord opened, that she attended unto the things which were spoken of Paul. And when she was baptized, and her household, she besought us, saying, If ye have judged me to be faithful to the Lord, come into my house, and abide there. And she constrained us. *(Acts 16:14-15)*

Let a man so account of us, as of the ministers of Christ, and stewards of the mysteries of God. Moreover it is required in stewards, that a man be found faithful. *(1 Corinthians 4:1-2)*

Now there are diversities of gifts, but the same Spirit. And there are differences of administrations, but the same Lord. And there are diversities of operations, but it is the same God which worketh all in all. But the manifestation of the Spirit is given to every man to profit withal. *(1 Corinthians 12:4-7)*

And God hath set some in the church, first apostles, secondarily prophets, thirdly teachers, after that miracles, then gifts of healings, helps, governments, diversities of tongues. Are all apostles? are all prophets? are all teachers? are all workers of miracles? have all the gifts of healing? do all speak with tongues? do all interpret? But covet earnestly the best gifts. *(1 Corinthians 12:28-31)*

I therefore, the prisoner of the Lord, beseech you that ye walk worthy of the vocation wherewith ye are called. With all lowliness and meekness, with long-suffering, forbearing one another in love; endeavoring to keep the unity of the spirit in the bond of peace. There is one body, and one Spirit, even as ye are called in one hope of your calling; one Lord, one faith, one baptism, one God and Father of all, who is above all, and through all, and in you all. But unto every one of us is given grace according to the measure of the gift of Christ. *(Ephesians 4:1-7)*

Paul and Timotheus, the servants of Jesus Christ, to all the saints in Christ Jesus which are at Philippi, with the bishops and deacons: Grace be unto you, and peace, from God our Father, and from the Lord Jesus Christ. I thank my God upon every remembrance of you, always in every prayer of mine for you all making request with joy, for your fellowship in the gospel from the first day until now; being confident for this very thing, that he which hath begun a good work in you will perform it until the day of Jesus Christ: even as it is meet for me to think this of you all, because I have you in my heart; inasmuch as both in my bonds, and in the defense and confirmation of the gospel, ye all are partakers of my grace. For God is my record, how greatly I long after you all. *(Philippians 1:1-8a)*

Therefore, my brethren dearly beloved and longed for, my joy and crown, so stand fast in the Lord, my dearly beloved. I beseech Euodias, and beseech Syntyche, that they be of the same mind in the Lord. And I entreat thee also, true yoke-fellow, help those women which labored with me in the gospel, with Clement also, and with other my fellow-laborers, whose names are in the book of life. Rejoice in the Lord alway: and again I say, Rejoice. *(Philippians 4:1-4)*

Likewise must the deacons be grave, not double tongued, not given to much wine; not greedy of filthy lucre; holding the mystery of the faith in a pure conscience. And let these also first be proved; then let them use the office of a deacon, being found blameless. *(1 Timothy 3:8-10)*

Let the elders that rule well be counted worthy of double honor, especially they who labor in the word and doctrine. *(1 Timothy 5:17)*

As every man hath received the gift, even so minister the same one to another, as good stewards of the manifold grace of God. *(1 Peter 4:10)*

Church

And Simon Peter answered and said, Thou art the Christ, the Son of the living God. And Jesus answered and said unto him, Blessed art thou, Simon Bar-jona: for flesh and blood hath not revealed it unto thee, but my Father which is in heaven. And I say also unto thee, That thou art Peter, and upon this rock I will build my church, and the gates of hell shall not prevail against it. *(Matthew 16:16-18)*

Again I say unto you, That if two of you shall agree on earth as touching any thing that they shall ask, it shall be done for them of my Father which is in heaven. For where two or three are gathered together in my name, there am I in the midst of them. *(Matthew 18:19-20)*

And he came to Nazareth, where he had been brought up: and, as his custom was, he went into the synagogue on the sabbath day, and stood up for to read. *(Luke 4:16)*

I am the vine, ye are the branches: He that abideth in me, and I in him, the same bringeth forth much fruit: for without me ye can do nothing. *(John 15:5)*

And when the day of Pentecost was fully come, they were all with one accord in one place. And suddenly there came a sound from heaven as of a rushing mighty wind, and it filled all the house where they were sitting. And there appeared unto them cloven tongues like as of fire, and it sat upon each of them. And they were all filled with the Holy Ghost, and began to speak with other tongues, as the Spirit gave them utterance. . . .

Then they that gladly received his word were baptized: and the same day there were added unto them about three thousand souls. And they continued stedfastly in the apostles' doctrine and fellowship, and in breaking of bread, and in prayers. . . .

And they, continuing daily with one accord in the temple, and breaking bread from house to house, did eat their meat with gladness and singleness of heart, praising God, and having favour with all the people. And the Lord added to the church daily such as should be saved. *(Acts 2:1-4,41-42,46-47)*

Let not then your good be evil spoken of: for the kingdom of God is not meat and drink; but righteousness, and peace and joy in the Holy Spirit. For he that in these things serveth Christ is acceptable to God, and approved of men. Let us therefore follow after the things which make for peace, and things wherewith one may edify another. *(Romans 14:16-19)*

For as the body is one, and hath many members, and all the members of that one body, being many, are one body: so also is Christ. For by one Spirit are we all baptized into one body, whether we be Jews or Gentiles, whether we be bond or free; and have been all made to drink into one Spirit. For the body is not one member, but many. If the foot shall say, Because I am not the hand, I am not of the body; is it therefore not of the body? And if the ear shall say, Because I am not the eye, I am not of the body; is it therefore not of the body? If the whole body were an eye, where were the hearing? If the whole were hearing, where were the smelling? But now hath God set the members every one of them in the body, as it hath pleased him. *(1 Corinthians 12:12-18)*

Wherefore I also, after I heard of your faith in the Lord Jesus, and love unto all the saints, cease not to give thanks for you, making mention of you in my prayers; that the God of our Lord Jesus Christ, the Father of glory, may give unto you the spirit of wisdom and revelation in the knowledge of him . . . and hath put all things under his feet, and gave him to be the head over all things to the church, which is his body, the fulness of him that filleth all in all. *(Ephesians 1:15-17,22-23)*

Now therefore ye are no more strangers and foreigners, but fellow-citizens with the saints, and of the household of God; and are built upon the foundation of the apostles and prophets, Jesus Christ himself being the chief corner stone; in whom all the building, fitly framed together, groweth unto a holy temple in the Lord: in whom ye also are builded together for a habitation of God through the Spirit. *(Ephesians 2:19-22)*

Put on the new man, which after God is created in righteousness and true holiness. Wherefore putting away lying, speak every man truth with his neighbor: for we are members one of another. *(Ephesians 4:24-25)*

And he is the head of the body, the church: who is the beginning, the firstborn from the dead; that in all things he might have the preeminence. *(Colossians 1:18)*

(Note: Also recommended is Revelation 1:4 through 3:22, containing the letters of John to the seven churches in Asia. Because of the length of this material, it is not reprinted here.)

The House of Worship

Blessed be thou, Lord God of Israel our father, for ever and ever. Thine, O Lord, is the greatness, and the power, and the glory, and the victory, and the majesty: for all that is in the heaven and in the earth is thine; thine is the kingdom, O Lord, and thou art exalted as head above all. Both riches and honor come of thee, and thou reignest over all; and in thine hand is power, and might; and in thine hand it is to make great, and to give strength unto all. Now therefore, our God, we thank thee, and praise thy glorious name. . . . For we are strangers before thee, and sojourners, as were all our fathers: our days on the earth are as a shadow, and there is none abiding. O Lord our God, all this store that we have prepared to build thee an house for thine holy name cometh of thine hand, and is all thine own. I know also, my God, that thou triest the heart, and hast pleasure in uprightness. As for me, in the uprightness of mine heart I have willingly offered all these things: and now have I seen with joy thy people, which are present here, to offer willingly unto thee. O Lord God of Abraham, Isaac, and of Israel, our fathers, keep this for ever in the imagination of the thoughts of the heart of thy people, and prepare their heart unto thee: and give . . . a perfect heart, to keep thy commandments, thy testimonies, and thy statutes. *(1 Chronicles 29:10-13,15-19)*

(Note: This and the following selection are sometimes used for the dedication of a building.)

The Lord hath said that he would dwell in the thick darkness. But I have built a house of habitation for thee, and a place for thy dwelling for ever. . . . Blessed be the Lord God of Israel, who hath with his hands fulfilled that which he spake with his mouth. . . . O Lord God of Israel, there is no God like thee in the heaven, nor in the earth; which keepest covenant, and showest mercy unto thy servants, that walk before thee with all their hearts. . . . Now, then, O Lord God of Israel, let thy word be verified, which thou hast

spoken unto thy servant David. But will God in very
deed dwell with men on the earth? Behold, heaven
and the heaven of heavens cannot contain thee; how
much less this house which I have built! Have respect
therefore to the prayer of thy servant, and to his
supplication, O Lord my God, to hearken unto the
cry and the prayer which thy servant prayeth before
thee: that thine eyes may be open upon this house day
and night, upon the place whereof thou hast said that thou
wouldst put thy name there; to hearken unto the prayer
which thy servant prayeth toward this place. . . .

Then hear thou from the heavens, even from thy
dwelling place, their prayer and their supplications,
and maintain their cause, and forgive thy people
which have sinned against thee.

Now, my God, let, I beseech thee, thy eyes be
open, and let thine ears be attent unto the prayer that
is made in this place. . . . Arise, O Lord God, into thy
resting place, thou, and the ark of thy strength: let thy
priests, O Lord God, be clothed with salvation, and
let thy saints rejoice in goodness. *(2 Chronicles 6:1-
2,4,14,17-20,39-41)*

One thing have I desired of the Lord, that will I
seek after; that I may dwell in the house of the Lord
all the days of my life, to behold the beauty of the
Lord, and to inquire in his temple. For in the time of
trouble he shall hide me in his pavilion: in the secret

of his tabernacle shall he hide me: he shall set me up upon a rock. *(Psalm 27:4-5)*

We have thought of thy lovingkindness, O God, in the midst of thy temple. According to thy name, O God, so is thy praise unto the ends of the earth: thy right hand is full of righteousness. Let mount Zion rejoice, let the daughters of Judah be glad, because of thy judgments. Walk about Zion, and go round about her: tell the towers thereof. Mark ye well her bulwarks, consider her palaces; that ye may tell it to the generation following. For this God is our God for ever and ever: he will be our guide even unto death. *(Psalm 48:9-14)*

How amiable are thy tabernacles, O Lord of hosts! My soul longeth, yea, even fainteth for the courts of the Lord: my heart and my flesh crieth out for the living God. Yea, the sparrow hath found a house, and the swallow a nest for herself, where she may lay her young, even thine altars, O Lord of hosts, my King, and my God. *(Psalm 84:1-3)*

O Lord God of hosts, hear my prayer: give ear, O God of Jacob. Behold, O God our shield, and look upon the face of thine anointed. For a day in thy courts is better than a thousand. I had rather be a doorkeeper in the house of my God, than to dwell in the tents of wickedness. For the Lord God is a sun and shield:

the Lord will give grace and glory; no good thing will he withhold from them that walk uprightly. O Lord of hosts, blessed is the man that trusteth in thee. *(Psalm 84:8-12)*

Make a joyful noise unto the Lord, all ye lands. Serve the Lord with gladness: come before his presence with singing. Know ye that the Lord he is God: it is he that hath made us, and not we ourselves; we are his people, and the sheep of his pasture. Enter into his gates with thanksgiving, and into his courts with praise: be thankful unto him, and bless his name. For the Lord is good; his mercy is everlasting, and his truth endureth to all generations. *(Psalm 100:1-5)*

I was glad when they said unto me, Let us go into the house of the Lord. . . . Peace be within thy walls, and prosperity within thy palaces. For my brethren and companions' sakes, I will now say, Peace be within thee. Because of the house of the Lord our God I will seek thy good. *(Psalm 122:1,7-9)*

Baptism

In those days came John the Baptist, preaching in the wilderness of Judea, and saying, Repent ye: for the kingdom of heaven is at hand. For this is he that was spoken of by the prophet Isaiah, saying, The voice of one crying in the wilderness, Prepare ye the way of the Lord, make his paths straight. And the same John had his raiment of camel's hair, and a leathern girdle about his loins; and his meat was locusts and wild honey. Then went out to him Jerusalem, and all Judea, and all the region round about Jordan, and were baptized of him in Jordan, confessing their sins.

Then cometh Jesus from Galilee to Jordan unto John, to be baptized of him. But John forbade him, saying, I have need to be baptized of thee, and comest thou to me? And Jesus answering said unto him, Suffer it to be so now: for thus it becometh us to fulfill all righteousness. Then he suffered him. And Jesus, when he was baptized, went up straightway out of the water: and lo, the heavens were opened unto him, and he saw the Spirit of God descending like a dove, and lighting upon him: and lo, a voice from heaven, saying, This is my beloved Son, in whom I am well pleased. *(Matthew 3:1-6,13-17)*

There was a man of the Pharisees, named Nicodemus, a ruler of the Jews: the same came to Jesus by night, and said unto him, Rabbi, we know that thou art a teacher come from God: for no man can do these miracles that thou doest, except God be with him. Jesus answered and said unto him, Verily, verily, I say unto thee, Except a man be born again, he cannot see the kingdom of God. Nicodemus saith unto him,

How can a man be born when he is old? can he enter the second time into his mother's womb, and be born? Jesus answered, Verily, verily, I say unto thee, Except a man be born of water and of the Spirit, he cannot enter into the kingdom of God. *(John 3:1-5)*

For John truly baptized with water; but ye shall be baptized with the Holy Ghost not many days hence. *(Acts 1:5)*

Then Peter said unto them, Repent, and be baptized every one of you in the name of Jesus Christ, for the remission of sins, and ye shall receive the gift of the Holy Ghost. For the promise is unto you, and to your children, and to all that are afar off, even as many as the Lord our God shall call. And with many other words did he testify and exhort, saying, Save yourselves from this untoward generation.

Then they that gladly received his word were baptized: and the same day there were added unto them about three thousand souls. And they continued stedfastly in the apostles' doctrine and fellowship, and in breaking of bread, and in prayers. *(Acts 2:38-42)*

And the angel of the Lord spake unto Philip, saying, Arise, and go toward the south, unto the way that goeth down from Jerusalem unto Gaza, which is desert. And he arose and went: and behold, a man of Ethiopia, an eunuch of great authority under Candace queen of the Ethiopians, who had the charge of all her treasure, and had come to Jerusalem for to worship, was returning, and sitting in his chariot read Isaiah the prophet. Then the Spirit said unto Philip, Go near, and join thyself to this chariot.

And Philip ran thither to him, and heard him read the prophet Isaiah, and said, Understandest thou what thou readest? And he said, How can I, except some man should guide me? And he desired Philip that he would come up, and sit with him. The place of the scripture which he read was this, He was led as a sheep to the slaughter: and like a lamb dumb before his shearer, so opened he not his mouth: in his humiliation his judgment was taken away: and who shall declare his generation? for his life is taken from the earth. And the eunuch answered Philip, and said, I pray thee, of whom speaketh the prophet this? of himself, or of some other man? Then Philip opened his mouth, and began at the same scripture, and preached unto him Jesus.

And as they went on their way they came unto a certain water: and the eunuch said, See, here is water; what doth hinder me to be baptized? And Philip said, If thou believest with all thy heart, thou mayest. And he answered and said, I believe that Jesus Christ is the son of God. And he commanded the chariot to stand still: and they went down both into the water, both Philip and the eunuch; and he baptized him. And when they were come up out of the water, the Spirit of the Lord caught away Philip, that the eunuch saw him no more: and he went on his way rejoicing. *(Acts 8:26-39)*

While Peter yet spake these words, the Holy Ghost fell on all them which heard the word. And they of the circumcision which believed, were astonished, as many as came with Peter, because that on the Gentiles also was poured out the gift of the Holy Ghost. For they heard them speak with tongues, and magnify God. Then answered Peter, Can any man forbid water, that these should not be baptized, which have received the Holy Ghost as well as we? And he commanded them to be baptized in the name of the Lord. *(Acts 10:44-48a)*

And on the sabbath we went out of the city by a river side, where prayer was wont to be made; and we sat down, and spake unto the women which resorted thither. And a certain woman named Lydia, a seller of purple, of the city of Thyatira, which worshipped God, heard us; whose heart the Lord opened, that she attended unto the things which were spoken of Paul. And when she was baptized, and her household, she besought us, saying, If ye have judged me to be faithful to the Lord, come into my house, and abide there. *(Acts 16:13-15)*

Know ye not, that so many of us as were baptized into Jesus Christ, were baptized into his death? Therefore we are buried with him by baptism into death: that like as Christ was raised up from the dead by the glory of the Father, even so we also should walk in newness of life. *(Romans 6:3-4)*

For as many of you as have been baptized into Christ, have put on Christ. *(Galatians 3:27)*

Buried with him in baptism, wherein also ye are risen with him through the faith of the operation of God, who hath raised him from the dead. *(Colossians 2:12)*

The Lord's Supper

Now the first day of the feast of unleavened bread, the disciples came to Jesus, saying unto him, Where wilt thou that we prepare for thee to eat the passover? And he said, Go into the city to such a man, and say unto him, The Master saith, My time is at hand; I will keep the passover at thy house with my disciples. And the disciples did as Jesus had appointed them, and they made ready the passover. Now when the even was come, he sat down with the twelve. And as they did eat, he said, Verily I say unto you, that one of you shall betray me. And they were exceeding sorrowful, and began every one of them to say unto him, Lord, is it I? And he answered and said, He that dippeth his hand with me in the dish, the same shall betray me. The Son of man goeth as it is written of him: but woe unto that man by whom the Son of man is betrayed! It had been good for that man if he had not been born. Then Judas, which betrayed him, answered and said, Master, is it I? He said unto him, Thou hast said.

And as they were eating, Jesus took bread and blessed it, and brake it, and gave it to the disciples, and said, Take, eat; this is my body. And he took the cup and gave thanks, and gave it to them, saying, Drink ye all of it; for this is my blood of the new testament, which is shed for many for the remission of sins. But I say unto you, I will not drink henceforth of this fruit of the vine, until that day when I drink it new with you in my Father's kingdom. And when they had sung a hymn, they went out into the mount of Olives. *(Matthew 26:17-30)*

Then Jesus said unto them, Verily, verily, I say unto you, Moses gave you not that bread from heaven; but my Father giveth you the true bread from heaven. For the bread of God is he which cometh down from heaven, and giveth life unto the world. Then said they unto him, Lord, evermore give us this bread. And Jesus said unto them, I am the bread of life: he that cometh to me shall never hunger; and he that believeth on me shall never thirst. *(John 6:32-35)*

Verily, verily, I say unto you, He that believeth on me hath everlasting life. I am that bread of life. This is the bread which cometh down from heaven, that a man may eat thereof, and not die. I am the living bread which came down from heaven: if any man eat of this bread, he shall live forever: and the bread that I will give is my flesh, which I will give for the life of the world. *(John 6:47-48,50-51)*

Then Jesus said unto them, Verily, verily, I say unto you, Except you eat the flesh of the Son of man, and drink his blood, ye have no life in you. Whoso eateth my flesh, and drinketh my blood, hath eternal life; and I will raise him up at the last day. For my flesh is meat indeed, and my blood is drink indeed. He that eateth my flesh, and drinketh my blood, dwelleth in me, and I in him. As the living Father hath sent me, and I live by the Father: so he that eateth me, even he shall live by me. This is that bread which came down from heaven: not as your fathers did eat manna, and are dead: he that eateth of this bread shall live for ever. *(John 6:53-58)*

I am the true vine, and my Father is the husbandman. Every branch in me that beareth not fruit he taketh away: and every branch that beareth fruit, he purgeth it, that it may bring forth more fruit. *(John 15:1-2)*

For I have received of the Lord that which also I

delivered unto you, That the Lord Jesus, the same night in which he was betrayed, took bread: and when he had given thanks, he brake it, and said, Take, eat: this is my body, which is broken for you: this do in remembrance of me. After the same manner, also he took the cup, when he had supped, saying, This cup is the new testament in my blood: this do ye, as oft as ye drink it, in remembrance of me. For as often as ye eat this bread, and drink this cup, ye do show the Lord's death till he come.

Wherefore, whosoever shall eat this bread, and drink this cup of the Lord, unworthily, shall be guilty of the body and blood of the Lord. But let a man examine himself, and so let him eat of that bread, and drink of that cup. *(1 Corinthians 11:23-28)*

Marriage

And the Lord God said, It is not good that the man should be alone; I will make him an help meet for him.

And Adam said, This is now bone of my bones, and flesh of my flesh: she shall be called Woman, because she was taken out of Man. Therefore shall a man leave his father and his mother, and shall cleave unto his wife: and they shall be one flesh. *(Genesis 2:18,23-24)*

Thou shalt not commit adultery. . . . Thou shalt not

covet thy neighbor's house, thou shalt not covet thy neighbor's wife, nor his manservant, nor his maidservant, nor his ox, nor his ass, nor anything that is thy neighbor's. *(Exodus 20:14,17)*

Blessed is the man that walketh not in the counsel of the ungodly, nor standeth in the way of sinners, nor sitteth in the seat of the scornful. But his delight is in the law of the Lord, and in his law doth he meditate day and night. *(Psalm 1:1-2)*

Whoso findeth a wife, findeth a good thing, and obtaineth favor of the Lord. *(Proverbs 18:22)*

Who can find a virtuous woman? for her price is far above rubies. The heart of her husband doth safely trust in her, so that he shall have no need of spoil. She will do him good and not evil all the days of her life. She seeketh wool, and flax, and worketh willingly with her hands. She is like the merchants' ships; she bringeth her food from afar. . . . She stretcheth out her hand to the poor; yea, she reacheth forth her hands to the needy.

Strength and honor are her clothing; and she shall rejoice in time to come. She openeth her mouth with wisdom; and in her tongue is the law of kindness. She looketh well to the ways of her household, and eateth not the bread of idleness. Her children arise up, and call her blessed; her husband also, and he praiseth

her. Many daughters have done virtuously, but thou
excellest them all. Favor is deceitful, and beauty is
vain: but a woman that feareth the Lord, she shall be
praised. *(Proverbs 31:10-14,20,25-30)*

Live joyfully with the wife whom thou lovest all
the days of the life of thy vanity, which he hath given
thee under the sun. *(Ecclesiastes 9:9a)*

For as a young man marrieth a virgin, so shall thy
sons marry thee: and as the bridegroom rejoiceth
over the bride, so shall thy God rejoice over thee.
(Isaiah 62:5)

And he answered and said unto them, Have ye not
read, that he which made them at the beginning, made
them male and female, and said, For this cause shall
a man leave father and mother, and shall cleave to his
wife; and they twain shall be one flesh? Wherefore,
they are no more twain, but one flesh. What therefore
God hath joined together, let no man put asunder.
(Matthew 19:4-6)

And the third day there was a marriage in Cana of
Galilee; and the mother of Jesus was there: and both
Jesus was called, and his disciples, to the marriage.
(John 2:1-2)

Let the husband render unto the wife due benevo-
lence: and likewise also the wife unto the husband.
(1 Corinthians 7:3)

Neither is the man without the woman, neither the woman without the man, in the Lord. For as the woman is of the man, even so is the man also by the woman; but all things of God. *(1 Corinthians 11:11-12)*

So ought men to love their wives as their own bodies. He that loveth his wife loveth himself. For no man ever yet hated his own flesh; but nourisheth and cherisheth it, even as the Lord the church: for we are members of his body, of his flesh, and of his bones. For this cause shall a man leave his father and mother, and shall be joined unto his wife, and they two shall be one flesh. This is a great mystery: but I speak concerning Christ and the church. Nevertheless, let every one of you in particular so love his wife even as himself; and the wife see that she reverence her husband. *(Ephesians 5:28-33)*

Children and Youth

And [Hagar] went and sat her down over against him, a good way off . . . for she said, Let me not see the death of the child. And she sat over against him, and lifted up her voice and wept. *(Genesis 21:16)*

For this child I prayed; and the Lord hath given me my petition which I asked of him; therefore also I have lent him to the Lord. *(1 Samuel 1:27-28)*

And the child did minister unto the Lord before

Eli the priest. *(1 Samuel 2:11b)*

Out of the mouth of babes and sucklings hast thou ordained strength because of thine enemies, that thou mightest still the enemy and the avenger. *(Psalm 8:2)*

Train up a child in the way he should go: and when he is old, he will not depart from it. *(Proverbs 22:6)*

The wolf shall also dwell with the lamb, and the leopard shall lie down with the kid; and the calf and the young lion and the fatling together; and a little child shall lead them. *(Isaiah 11:6)*

And Jesus called a little child unto him and set him in the midst of them, and said, Verily I say unto you, except ye be converted and become as little children, ye shall not enter into the kingdom of heaven. Whosoever therefore shall humble himself as this little child, the same is greatest in the kingdom of heaven. *(Matthew 18:2-4)*

Take heed that ye despise not one of these little ones; for I say unto you, That in heaven their angels do always behold the face of my Father which is in heaven. *(Matthew 18:10)*

And he took a child and set him in the midst of them; and when he had taken him in his arms, he said unto them, Whosoever shall receive one of such children in my name receiveth me; and whosoever receiveth me, receiveth not me, but him that sent me. *(Mark 9:36-37)*

And they brought young children to him that he should touch them: and his disciples rebuked them that brought them. But when Jesus saw it, he was much displeased, and said unto them, Suffer the little children to come unto me, and forbid them not; for of such is the kingdom of God. Verily, I say unto you, whosoever shall not receive the kingdom of God as a little child, he shall not enter therein. And he took them up in his arms, put his hands upon them, and blessed them. *(Mark 10:13-16)*

When he was twelve years old, they went up to Jerusalem after the custom of the feast. And when they had fulfilled the days, as they returned, the child Jesus tarried behind in Jerusalem; and Joseph and his mother knew not of it. But they, supposing him to have been in the company, went a day's journey; and they sought him among their kinsfolk and acquaintance. And when they found him not, they turned back again to Jerusalem, seeking him.

And it came to pass, that after three days they found him in the temple, sitting in the midst of the doctors, both hearing them, and asking them questions. And all that heard him were astonished at his understanding and answers. And when they saw him, they were amazed: and his mother said unto him,

Son, why hast thou thus dealt with us? behold, thy father and I have sought thee sorrowing. And he said unto them, How is it that ye sought me? wist ye not that I must be about my Father's business? . . . And Jesus increased in wisdom and stature, and in favor with God and man. *(Luke 2:42-49,52)*

When I was a child, I spake as a child, I understood as a child, I thought as a child: but when I became a man, I put away childish things. *(1 Corinthians 13:11)*

Children, obey your parents in all things: for this is well pleasing unto the Lord. *(Colossians 3:20)*

Let no man despise thy youth; but be thou an example of the believers, in word, in conversation, in charity, in spirit, in faith, in purity. Till I come, give attendance to reading, to exhortation, to doctrine. *(1 Timothy 4:12)*

Temperance

Do not drink wine nor strong drink, thou nor thy sons with thee, when ye go into the tabernacle of the congregation, lest ye die. It shall be a statute forever throughout your generations. *(Leviticus 10:9)*

Wine is a mocker, strong drink is raging; and whosoever is deceived thereby is not wise. *(Proverbs 20:1)*

Be not among winebibbers; among riotous eaters of flesh. For the drunkard and the glutton shall come to poverty: and drowsiness shall clothe a man with rags. *(Proverbs 23:20-21)*

Who hath woe? who hath sorrow? who hath contentions? who hath babbling? who hath wounds without cause? who hath redness of eyes? They that tarry long at the wine; they that go to seek mixed wine. Look not thou upon the wine when it is red, when it giveth his color in the cup, when it moveth itself aright. At the last it biteth like a serpent, and stingeth like an adder. *(Proverbs 23:29-32)*

Woe unto them that rise up early in the morning, that they may follow strong drink; that continue until night, till wine inflame them! And the harp, and the viol, the tabret, and pipe, and wine, are in their feasts: but they regard not the work of the Lord, neither consider the operation of his hands. . . . Woe unto them that are mighty to drink wine, and men of strength to mingle strong drink: which justify the wicked for reward, and take away the righteousness of the righteous from him! *(Isaiah 5:11-12,22-23)*

Woe to the crown of pride, to the drunkards of Ephraim, whose glorious beauty is a fading flower, which are on the head of the fat valleys of them that are overcome with wine! . . . The crown of pride, the

drunkards of Ephraim, shall be trodden under feet. . . .
They also have erred through wine, and through
strong drink are out of the way. The priests and the
prophet have erred through strong drink, they are
swallowed up of wine, they are out of the way
through strong drink; they err in vision, they stumble
in judgment. *(Isaiah 28:1,3,7)*

Woe unto him that giveth his neighbor drink, that
puttest thy bottle to him, and makest him drunken
also, that thou mayest look on their nakedness!
(Habakkuk 2:15)

It is good neither to eat flesh nor to drink wine,
nor anything whereby thy brother stumbleth, or is
offended, or is made weak. *(Romans 14:21)*

And every man that striveth for the mastery is
temperate in all things. *(1 Corinthians 9:25a)*

But speak thou the things which become sound
doctrine: That the aged men be sober, grave, temperate, sound in faith, in charity, in patience. The aged
women, likewise, that they be in behavior as becometh holiness, not false accusers, not given to
much wine, teachers of good things; that they may
teach the young women to be sober, to love their
husbands, to love their children. Young men likewise
exhort to be sober minded. *(Titus 2:1-4,6)*

Readings for the Sick and Shut-in

The Lord is my shepherd; I shall not want. He maketh me to lie down in green pastures: he leadeth me beside the still waters. He restoreth my soul: he leadeth me in the paths of righteousness for his name's sake. Yea, though I walk through the valley of the shadow of death, I will fear no evil: for thou art with me; thy rod and thy staff they comfort me. Thou preparest a table before me in the presence of mine enemies: thou anointest my head with oil; my cup runneth over. Surely goodness and mercy shall follow me all the days of my life: and I will dwell in the house of the Lord forever. *(Psalm 23:1-6)*

God is our refuge and strength, a very present help in trouble. Therefore will not we fear, though the earth be removed, and though the mountains be carried into the midst of the sea; though the waters thereof roar and be troubled, though the mountains shake with the swelling thereof.

There is a river, the streams whereof shall make glad the city of God, the holy place of the tabernacles of the most High. God is in the midst of her; she shall not be moved: God shall help her, and that right early.

The heathen raged, the kingdoms were moved: he uttered his voice, the earth melted. The Lord of hosts is with us; the God of Jacob is our refuge. *(Psalm 46:1-7)*

He that dwelleth in the secret place of the most High shall abide under the shadow of the Almighty. I will say of the Lord, He is my refuge and my fortress: my God; in him will I trust. . . .

Thou shalt not be afraid for the terror by night; nor for the arrow that flieth by day; nor for the pestilence that walketh in darkness; nor for the destruction that wasteth at noonday. . . .

There shall no evil befall thee, neither shall any plague come nigh thy dwelling. For he shall give his angels charge over thee, to keep thee in all thy ways. *(Psalm 91:1-2,5-6,10-11)*

Bless the Lord, O my soul: and all that is within me, bless his holy name. Bless the Lord, O my soul, and forget not all his benefits: who forgiveth all thine iniquities; who healeth all thy diseases; who redeemeth thy life from destruction; who crowneth thee with lovingkindness and tender mercies. . . .

The Lord is merciful and gracious, slow to anger, and plenteous in mercy. He will not always chide: neither will he keep his anger forever. He hath not dealt with us after our sins; nor rewarded us according to our iniquities. For as the heaven is high above the earth, so great is his mercy toward them that fear him. As far as the east is from the west, so far hath he removed our transgressions from us. Like as a father pitieth his children, so the Lord pitieth them that fear him. *(Psalm 103:1-4,8-13)*

I will lift up mine eyes unto the hills, from whence cometh my help. My help cometh from the Lord, which made heaven and earth. He will not suffer thy foot to be moved: he that keepeth thee will not slumber. Behold, he that keepeth Israel shall neither slumber nor sleep. The Lord is thy keeper: the Lord is thy shade upon thy right hand. The sun shall not smite thee by day, nor the moon by night. The Lord shall preserve thee from all evil: he shall preserve thy soul. The Lord shall preserve thy going out and thy coming in from this time forth, and even for evermore. *(Psalm 121:1-8)*

O Lord, by these things men live, and in all these things is the life of my spirit: so wilt thou recover me and make me to live. Behold, for peace I had great bitterness: but thou hast in love to my soul delivered it from the pit of corruption; for thou hast cast all my sins behind thy back. *(Isaiah 38:16-17)*

And Jesus went about all Galilee, teaching in their synagogues, and preaching the gospel of the kingdom, and healing all manner of sickness and all manner of disease among the people. *(Matthew 4:23)*

Come unto me, all ye that labor and are heavy laden, and I will give you rest. Take my yoke upon you, and learn of me; for I am meek and lowly in heart: and ye shall find rest unto your souls. For my yoke is easy, and my burden is light. *(Matthew 11:28-30)*

For God so loved the world, that he gave his only begotten Son, that whosoever believeth in him should not perish, but have everlasting life. *(John 3:16)*

Let not your heart be troubled: ye believe in God, believe also in me. In my Father's house are many mansions: if it were not so, I would have told you. I go to prepare a place for you. *(John 14:1-2)*

For I reckon that the sufferings of this present time are not worthy to be compared with the glory which shall be revealed in us. . . . And we know that all things work together for good to them that love God, to them who are the called according to his purpose. *(Romans 8:18,28)*

Who shall separate us from the love of Christ? shall tribulation, or distress, or persecution, or famine, or nakedness, or peril, or sword? . . . Nay, in all these things we are more than conquerors through him that loved us. For I am persuaded, that neither death, nor life, nor angels, nor principalities, nor powers, nor things present, nor things to come, nor height, nor depth, nor any other creature, shall be able to separate us from the love of God, which is in Christ Jesus, our Lord. *(Romans 8:35,37-39)*

Death and Eternal Life

I know that my Redeemer liveth, and that he shall stand at the latter day upon the earth. *(Job 19:25)*

Thou shalt guide me with thy counsel and afterward receive me to glory. Whom have I in heaven but thee? and there is none upon earth that I desire besides thee. My flesh and my heart faileth: but God is the strength of my heart, and my portion for ever. *(Psalm 73:24-26)*

I will ransom them from the power of the grave; I will redeem them from death: O death, I will be thy plagues; O grave, I will be thy destruction. *(Hosea 13:14)*

As touching the dead, that they rise: have ye not read in the book of Moses, how in the bush God spake unto him, saying, I am the God of Abraham, and the God of Isaac, and the God of Jacob? He is not the God of the dead, but the God of the living. *(Mark 12:26-27a)*

Verily, verily, I say unto you, The hour is coming, and now is, when the dead shall hear the voice of the Son of God; and they that hear shall live. For as the Father hath life in himself; so hath he given to the Son to have life in himself; and hath given him authority to execute judgment also, because he is the

Son of man. *(John 5:25-27)*

Let not your heart be troubled: ye believe in God, believe also in me. In my Father's house are many mansions: if it were not so I would have told you. I go to prepare a place for you. And if I go and prepare a place for you, I will come again, and receive you unto myself; that where I am there ye may be also. *(John 14:1-3)*

So also is the resurrection of the dead. It is sown in corruption, it is raised in incorruption; it is sown in dishonor, it is raised in glory: it is sown in weakness, it is raised in power: it is sown a natural body, it is raised a spiritual body. There is a natural body, and there is a spiritual body. And so it is written, The first man Adam was made a living soul; the last Adam was made a quickening spirit.

Howbeit, that was not first which is spiritual, but that which is natural; and afterward that which is spiritual. The first man is of the earth, earthy: the second man is the Lord from heaven. As is the earthy, such are they also that are earthy: and as is the heavenly, such are they also that are heavenly. And as we have borne the image of the earthy, we shall also bear the image of the heavenly. *(1 Corinthians 15:42-49)*

So when this corruptible shall have put on incorruption, and this mortal shall have put on immortality, then shall be brought to pass the saying that is written, Death is swallowed up in victory. O death, where is thy sting? O grave, where is thy victory? The sting of death is sin; and the strength of sin is the law.

But thanks be to God, which giveth us the victory through our Lord Jesus Christ. Therefore, my beloved brethren, be ye stedfast, unmoveable, always abounding in the work of the Lord, forasmuch as ye know that your labor is not in vain in the Lord. *(1 Corinthians 15:54-58)*

For which cause we faint not; but though our outward man perish, yet the inward man is renewed day by day. For our light affliction, which is but for a moment, worketh for us a far more exceeding and eternal weight of glory; while we look not at the things which are seen, but at the things which are not seen: for the things which are seen are temporal; but the things which not seen are eternal. *(2 Corinthians 4:16-18)*

For we know that if our earthly house of this tabernacle were dissolved, we have a building of God, a house not made with hands, eternal in the heavens. . . . Therefore we are always confident, knowing that, whilst we are at home in the body, we are absent from the Lord. . . . We are confident, I say, and willing rather to be absent from the body, and to be present with the Lord. Wherefore we labor that, whether present or absent, we may be accepted of him. *(2 Corinthians 5:1,6,8-9)*

Yea, doubtless, and I count all things but loss for the excellency of the knowledge of Christ Jesus my Lord. . . . that I may know him, and the power of his resurrection, and the fellowship of his sufferings, being made conformable unto his death; if by any means I might attain unto the resurrection of the dead. *(Philippians 3:8a,10-11)*

If ye then be risen with Christ, seek those which are above, where Christ sitteth at the right hand of God. Set your affection on things above, not on things on the earth. For ye are dead, and your life is hid with Christ in God. When Christ, who is our life, shall appear, then shall ye also appear with him in glory. *(Colossians 3:1-4)*

I would not have you to be ignorant, brethren, concerning them which are asleep, that ye sorrow not even as others which have no hope. For if we believe that Jesus died and rose again, even so them also which sleep in Jesus, will God bring with him. For this we say unto you by the word of the Lord, that we which are alive and remain unto the coming of the Lord shall not prevent them which are asleep. *(1 Thessalonians 4:13-15)*

For I am now ready to be offered, and the time of my departure is at hand. I have fought a good fight, I have finished my course, I have kept the faith; henceforth there is laid up for me a crown of right-eousness, which the Lord, the righteous judge, shall give me at that day: and not to me only, but unto all them also that love his appearing. *(2 Timothy 4:6-8)*

Grief

When David saw that his servants whispered, David perceived that the child was dead: therefore David said unto his servants: Is the child dead? And they said, He is dead. Then David arose from the earth, and washed, and anointed himself, and changed his apparel, and came into the house of the Lord, and worshiped: then he came to his own house; and when he required, they set bread before him, and he did eat. Then said his servants unto him, What thing is this that thou hast done? thou didst fast and weep for the child, while it was alive; but when the child was dead, thou didst rise and eat bread. And he said, While the child was yet alive, I fasted and wept: for I said, Who can tell whether God will be gracious to me, that the child may live? But now he is dead, wherefore should I fast? can I bring him back again? I shall go to him, but he shall not return to me. *(2 Samuel 12:19-23)*

Unto thee, O Lord, do I lift up my soul. . . . Turn thee unto me, and have mercy upon me; for I am desolate and afflicted. The troubles of my heart are enlarged. O bring thou me out of my distress. Look upon mine affliction and my pain; and forgive all my sins. *(Psalm 25:1,16-18)*

O my God, my soul is cast down within me. . . . All thy waves and thy billows are gone over me. *(Psalm 42:6a,7b)*

Out of the depths have I cried unto thee, O Lord. Lord, hear my voice: let thine ears be attentive to the voice of my supplications. . . . I wait for the Lord, my soul doth wait, and in his word do I hope. My soul waiteth for the Lord more than they that watch for the morning: I say, more than they that watch for the morning. *(Psalm 130:1-2, 5-6)*

Is it nothing to you, all ye that pass by? behold and see if there be any sorrow like unto my sorrow, which is done unto me, wherewith the Lord hath afflicted me? *(Lamentations 1:12)*

The Lord will not cast off forever. But though he cause grief, yet will he have compassion, according to the multitude of his mercies. For he doth not afflict willingly, nor grieve the children of men. *(Lamentations 3:31-33)*

Comfort

Like as a father pitieth his children, so the Lord pitieth them that fear him. For he knoweth our frame; he remembereth that we are dust. *(Psalm 103:13-14)*

Gracious is the Lord, and righteous, yea, our God is merciful. . . . I was brought low, and he helped me. This is my comfort in my affliction. *(Psalm 116:5,6b; 119:50a)*

Comfort ye, comfort ye my people, saith your God. *(Isaiah 40:1)*

Blessed are they that mourn, for they shall be comforted. *(Matthew 5:4)*

While [Jesus] yet spake, there came from the ruler of the synagogue's house certain which said, Thy daughter is dead; why troublest thou the Master any further? As soon as Jesus heard the word that was spoken, he saith unto the ruler of the synagogue, Be not afraid, only believe. *(Mark 5:35-36)*

The spirit itself beareth witness with our spirit, that we are the children of God: and if children, then heirs: heirs of God, and joint-heirs with Christ; if so be that we suffer with him, that we may be also glorified together. For I reckon that the sufferings of this present time are not worthy to be compared with the glory which shall be revealed in us. *(Romans 8:16-18)*

Blessed be God, even the Father of our Lord Jesus Christ, the Father of mercies, and the God of all comfort; who comforteth us in all our tribulations, that we may be able to comfort them which are in any trouble, by the comfort wherewith we ourselves are comforted of God.

For as the sufferings of Christ abound in us, so our consolation also aboundeth by Christ. And whether we be afflicted, it is for your consolation and salvation, which is effectual in the enduring of the same sufferings which we also suffer: or whether we be comforted, it is for your consolation and salvation. And our hope of you is stedfast, knowing, that as ye are partakers of the sufferings, so shall ye be also of the consolation. *(2 Corinthians 1:3-7)*

And one of the elders answered, saying unto me, What are these which are arrayed in white robes? and whence came they? And I said unto him, Sir, thou knowest. And he said to me, These are they which came out of great tribulation, and have washed their robes, and made them white in the blood of the Lamb.

Therefore are they before the throne of God, and serve him day and night in his temple: and he that sitteth on the throne shall dwell among them. They shall hunger no more, neither thirst any more; neither shall the sun light on them, nor any heat. For the Lamb which is in the midst of the throne shall feed them, and shall lead them unto living fountains of waters: and God shall wipe away all tears from their eyes. *(Revelation 7:13-17)*

And I saw a new heaven and a new earth: for the first heaven and the first earth were passed away; and there was no more sea. And I John saw the holy city, new Jerusalem, coming down from God out of heaven, prepared as a bride adorned for her husband.

And I heard a great voice out of heaven saying, Behold, the tabernacle of God is with men, and he will dwell with them, and they shall be his people, and God himself shall be with them, and be their God. And God shall wipe away all tears from their eyes; and there shall be no more death, neither sorrow, nor crying, neither shall there be any more pain: for the former things are passed away.

And he that sat upon the throne said, Behold, I make all things new. And he said unto me, Write: for these words are true and faithful. *(Revelation 21:1-5)*

The Holy Scriptures

Man doth not live by bread only, but by every word that proceedeth out of the mouth of the Lord doth man live. *(Deuteronomy 8:3b)*

How sweet are thy words unto my taste! yea, sweeter than honey to my mouth! Through thy precepts I get understanding: therefore I hate every false way. Thy word is a lamp unto my feet, and a light unto my path. *(Psalm 119:103-105)*

Seek ye out of the book of the Lord, and read. *(Isaiah 34:16a)*

Jesus answered and said unto them, Ye do err, not knowing the scriptures, nor the power of God. *(Matthew 22:29)*

And they said to one another, Did not our heart burn within us, while he talked with us by the way, and while he opened to us the scriptures? *(Luke 24:32)*

Search the scriptures, for in them ye think ye have eternal life: and they are they which testify of me. *(John 5:39)*

For whatsoever things were written aforetime were written for our learning, that we through patience and comfort of the scriptures might have hope. *(Romans 15:4)*

For we have not followed cunningly devised fables, when we made known unto you the power and coming of our Lord Jesus Christ, but were eyewitnesses of his majesty. For he received from God the Father honor and glory, when there came such a voice to him from the excellent glory, This is my beloved

Son, in whom I am well pleased. And this voice which came from heaven we heard, when we were with him in the holy mount. We have also a more sure word of prophecy; whereunto ye do well that ye take heed, as unto a light that shineth in a dark place, until the day dawn, and the day star arise in your hearts: knowing this first, that no prophecy of the scripture is of any private interpretation. For the prophecy came not in old time by the will of man: but holy men of God spake as they were moved by the Holy Ghost. *(2 Peter 1:16-21)*

The Birth of Christ

And it came to pass in those days, that there went out a decree from Caesar Augustus, that all the world should be taxed. And all went to be taxed, every one to his own city. And Joseph also went up from Galilee, out of the city of Nazareth, into Judea, unto the city of David, which is called Bethlehem; (because he was of the house and lineage of David:) to be taxed with Mary his espoused wife, being great with child.

And so it was, that, while they were there, the days were accomplished that she should be delivered. And she brought forth her firstborn son, and wrapped him in swaddling clothes, and laid him in a manger, because there was no room for them in the inn.

And there were in the same country shepherds abiding in the field, keeping watch over their flock by night. And, lo, the angel of the Lord came upon them, and the glory of the Lord shone round about them: and they were sore afraid. And the angel said unto them, Fear not: for, behold I bring you good tidings of great joy, which shall be to all people. For unto you is born this day in the city of David a Savior, which is Christ the Lord. And this shall be a sign unto you; Ye shall find the babe wrapped in swaddling clothes, lying in a manger. And suddenly there was with the angel a multitude of the heavenly host praising God, and saying, Glory to God in the highest, and on earth peace, good will toward men.

And it came to pass, as the angels were gone away from them into heaven, the shepherds said one to another, Let us now go even unto Bethlehem, and see this thing which is come to pass, which the Lord hath made known unto us. And they came with haste, and found Mary and Joseph, and the babe lying in a manger.

And when they had seen it, they made known abroad the saying which was told them concerning this child. And all they that heard it wondered at those things which were told them by the shepherds. But Mary kept all these things, and pondered them in her heart. And the shepherds returned, glorifying and praising God for all the things that they had heard and seen, as it was told unto them. *(Luke 2:1,3-20)*

The Beatitudes of Christ

Blessed are the poor in spirit: for theirs is the kingdom of heaven.

Blessed are they that mourn: for they shall be comforted.

Blessed are the meek: for they shall inherit the earth.

Blessed are they which do hunger and thirst after righteousness: for they shall be filled.

Blessed are the merciful: for they shall obtain mercy.

Blessed are the pure in heart: for they shall see God.

Blessed are the peacemakers: for they shall be called the children of God.

Blessed are they which are persecuted for right-eousness' sake: for theirs is the kingdom of heaven.

Blessed are ye, when men shall revile you, and persecute you, and shall say all manner of evil against you falsely, for my sake. Rejoice, and be exceeding glad, for great is your reward in heaven: for so persecuted they the prophets which were before you. *(Matthew 5:3-12)*

The Cross of Christ

And when they were come to the place, which is called Calvary, there they crucified him, and the malefactors, one on the right hand and the other on the left. Then said Jesus, Father, forgive them, for they know not what they do. And they parted his raiment, and cast lots. And the people stood beholding. And the rulers also with them derided him, saying, He saved others, let him save himself, if he be Christ, the chosen of God. And the soldiers also mocked him, coming to him, and offering him vinegar, and saying, If thou be the king of the Jews, save thyself. And a superscription also was written over him in letters of Greek, and Latin, and Hebrew, THIS IS THE KING OF THE JEWS.

. . . And it was about the sixth hour, and there was a darkness over all the earth until the ninth hour. And the sun was darkened, and the veil of the temple was rent in the midst. And when Jesus had cried with a loud voice, he said, Father, into thy hands I commend my spirit: and having said thus, he gave up the ghost. *(Luke 23:33-38,44-46)*

Then Peter and the other apostles answered and said, We ought to obey God rather than men. The God of our fathers raised up Jesus, whom ye slew and hanged on a tree. Him hath God exalted with his right hand to be a Prince and a Savior, for to give repentance to Israel, and forgiveness of sins. And we are his witnesses of these things; and so is also the Holy Ghost, whom God hath given to them that obey them. *(Acts 5:29-32)*

But we preach Christ crucified, unto the Jews a stumblingblock, and unto the Greeks foolishness; But unto them which are called, both Jews and Greeks, Christ the power of God, and the wisdom of God. Because the foolishness of God is wiser than men; and the weakness of God is stronger than men. *(1 Corinthians 1:23-25)*

For I determined not to know anything among you, save Jesus Christ, and him crucified. *(1 Corinthians 2:2)*

I am crucified with Christ: nevertheless I live; yet not I, but Christ liveth in me: and the life which I now live in the flesh I live by the faith of the Son of God, who loved me, and gave himself for me. *(Galatians 2:20)*

But God forbid that I should glory, save in the cross of our Lord Jesus Christ, by whom the world is crucified unto me, and I unto the world. *(Galatians 6:14)*

But now in Christ Jesus ye who sometimes were far off are made nigh by the blood of Christ. For he is our peace, who hath made both one, and hath broken down the middle wall of partition between us; having abolished in his flesh the enmity, even the law of commandments contained in ordinances; for to make in himself of twain one new man, so making peace; and that he might reconcile both unto God in one body by the cross, having slain the enmity thereby: and came and preached peace to you which were afar off, and to them that were nigh. *(Ephesians 2:13-17)*

Let this mind be in you, which was also in Christ Jesus: Who, being in the form of God, thought it not robbery to be equal with God: but made of himself no reputation, and took upon him the form of a servant, and was made in the likeness of men: and being found in fashion as a man, he humbled himself, and became obedient unto death, even the death of the cross.

Wherefore God also hath highly exalted him, and given him a name which is above every name: that at the name of Jesus every knee should bow, of things in heaven, and things in earth, and things under the earth; and that every tongue should confess that Jesus Christ is Lord, to the glory of God the Father. *(Philippians 2:5-11)*

For there is one God, and one mediator between God and men, the man Christ Jesus; who gave himself a ransom for all, to be testified in due time. *(1 Timothy 2:5-6)*

Hereby perceive we the love of God, because he laid down his life for us: and we ought to lay down our lives for the brethren. *(1 John 3:16)*

The Resurrection of Christ

In the end of the sabbath, as it began to dawn toward the first day of the week, came Mary Magdalene and the other Mary to see the sepulchre. And, behold, there was a great earthquake: for the angel of the Lord descended from heaven, and came and rolled back the stone from the door, and sat upon it. His countenance was like lightning, and his raiment white as snow: and for fear of him the keepers did shake, and became as dead men.

And the angel answered and said unto the women, Fear not ye: for I know that ye seek Jesus, which was crucified. He is not here: for he is risen, as he said. Come, see the place where the Lord lay. And go quickly, and tell his disciples that he is risen from the dead; and, behold, he goeth before you into Galilee; there shall ye see him: lo, I have told you .

And they departed quickly from the sepulchre with fear and great joy; and did run to bring his disciples word. And as they went to tell his disciples, behold, Jesus met them, saying, All hail. And they came and held him by the feet, and worshiped him. Then said Jesus unto them, Be not afraid: go tell my brethren that they go into Galilee, and there shall they see me. *(Matthew 28:1-10)*

For if we have been planted together in the likeness of his death, we shall be also in the likeness of his resurrection: knowing this, that our old man is crucified with him, that the body of sin might be destroyed, that henceforth we should not serve sin. For he that is dead is freed from sin.

Now if we be dead with Christ, we believe that we shall also live with him: knowing that Christ being raised from the dead dieth no more; death hath no more dominion over him. For in that he died, he died unto sin once: but that in that he liveth, he liveth unto God. Likewise reckon ye also yourselves to be dead indeed unto sin, but alive unto God through Jesus Christ our Lord. *(Romans 6:5-11)*

Now if Christ be preached that he rose from the dead, how say some among you that there is no resurrection of the dead? But if there be no resurrection of the dead, then is Christ not risen: and if Christ be not risen, then is our preaching vain, and your faith is also vain. Yea, and we are found false witnesses of God; because we have testified of God that he raised up Christ: whom he raised not up, if so be that the dead rise not.

For if the dead rise not, then is not Christ raised: and if Christ be not raised, your faith is vain; ye are yet in your sins. Then they also which are fallen asleep in Christ are perished. If in this life only we have hope in Christ, we are of all men most miserable. But now is Christ risen from the dead, and become the firstfruits of them that slept. *(1 Corinthians 15:12-20)*

O death, where is thy sting? O grave, where is thy victory? The sting of death is sin; and the strength of sin is the law. But thanks be to God, which giveth us the victory through our Lord Jesus Christ. *(1 Corinthians 15:55-57)*

Benedictions

The Lord bless thee, and keep thee; the Lord make his face to shine upon thee, and be gracious upon thee; the Lord lift up his countenance upon thee, and give thee peace. *(Numbers 6:24-26)*

The grace of our Lord Jesus Christ be with you all. Amen. *(Romans 16:24)*

To God only wise, be glory through Jesus Christ for ever. Amen. *(Romans 16:27)*

Grace be unto you, and peace, from God our

Father, and from the Lord Jesus Christ. *(1 Corinthians 1:3)*

The grace of the Lord Jesus Christ, and the love of God, and the communion of the Holy Ghost, be with you all. Amen. *(2 Corinthians 13:14)*

Brethren, the grace of our Lord Jesus Christ be with your spirit. Amen. *(Galatians 6:18)*

Peace be to the brethren, and love with faith, from God the Father and the Lord Jesus Christ. Grace be with all them that love our Lord Jesus Christ in sincerity. Amen. *(Ephesians 6:23-24)*

The peace of God which passeth all understanding, shall keep your hearts and minds through Christ Jesus. . . . Now unto God and our Father be glory for ever and ever. Amen. *(Philippians 4:7,20)*

Grace, mercy, and peace, from God the Father and Christ Jesus our Lord. *(2 Timothy 1:2)*

Grace to you, and peace, from God our Father and the Lord Jesus Christ. *(Philemon 3)*

Now the God of peace, that brought again from the dead our Lord Jesus, that great shepherd of the sheep, through the blood of the everlasting covenant, make you perfect in every good work to do his will, working in you that which is well-pleasing in his sight, through Jesus Christ; to whom be glory for ever and ever. Amen. *(Hebrews 13:20-21)*

Grace and peace be multiplied unto you through the knowledge of God, and of Jesus our Lord. *(2 Peter 1:2)*

Grace be with you, mercy, and peace, from God the Father, and from the Lord Jesus Christ, the Son of the Father, in truth and love. *(2 John 3)*

Now unto him that is able to keep you from falling, and to present you faultless before the presence of his glory with exceeding joy, to the only wise God our Saviour, be glory and majesty, dominion and power, both now and ever. Amen. *(Jude 24-25)*

The grace of our Lord Jesus Christ be with you all. Amen. *(Revelation 22:21)*

III

The Marriage Service

III

The Marriage Service

A Traditional Marriage Service Based on that of the Episcopal Church

Address

At the day and time appointed for Solemnization of Matrimony, the persons to be married shall come into the body of the church, or shall be ready in some proper house, with their friends and neighbors; and there standing together, the man on the right hand, and the woman on the left, the Minister shall say:

Dearly beloved, we are gathered together here in the sight of God, and in the face of this company, to join together this man and this woman in holy matrimony; which is an honorable estate, instituted of God, signifying unto us the mystical union that is betwixt Christ and his church: which holy estate Christ adorned and beautified with his presence and first miracle that he wrought in Cana of Galilee, and is commended of Saint Paul to be honorable among all: and therefore is not by any to be entered into unadvisedly or lightly; but reverently, discreetly, advisedly, soberly, and in the fear of God. Into this holy estate these two persons present come now to be joined. If anyone can show just cause why they may not lawfully be joined together, let him now speak, or else hereafter forever hold his peace.

Charge

And also speaking unto the persons who are to be married, the minister shall say:

I require and charge you both, as ye will answer at the dreadful day of judgment when the secrets of all hearts shall be disclosed, that if either of you know any impediment, why ye may not be lawfully joined together in matrimony, ye do now confess it. For be ye well assured, that if any persons are joined together otherwise than as God's Word doth allow, their marriage is not lawful.

Vows

The Minister shall say to the man:

_____, wilt thou have this woman to thy wedded wife, to live together after God's ordinance in the holy estate of matrimony? Wilt thou love her, comfort her, honor and keep her in sickness and in health; and, forsaking all others, keep thee only unto her, so long as ye both shall live?

The man: I will.

Then shall the Minister say unto the woman:

_____, wilt thou have this man to thy wedded husband, to live together after God's ordinance in the holy estate of matrimony? Wilt thou love him, comfort him, honor and keep him in sickness and in health; and, forsaking all others, keep thee only unto him, so long as ye both shall live?

The woman: I will.

Then shall the Minister say:

Who giveth this woman to be married to this man?

Father's reply: Her mother and I do.

Then shall they give their troth to each other in this manner: the Minister, receiving the woman at her father's hands, shall cause the man with his right hand to take the woman by her right hand, and to say after him as followeth:

I _____ take thee _____ to my wedded wife, to have and to hold from this day forward, for better or for worse, for richer or for poorer, in sickness and in health, to love and to cherish, till death us do part, according to God's holy ordinance; and thereto I plight thee my troth.

Then shall they loose their hands; and the woman with her right hand taking the man by his right hand, shall likewise say after the Minister:

I _____ take thee _____ to my wedded husband, to have and to hold from this day forward, for better or for worse, for richer or for poorer, in sickness and in health, to love and to cherish, till death us do part, according to God's holy ordinance; and thereto I give thee my troth.

Presentation of the Ring(s)

Then shall they again loose their hands; and the man shall give unto the woman a ring on this wise: the Minister, taking the ring, shall deliver it unto the man, to put it upon the fourth finger of the woman's left hand. And the man holding the ring there, and taught by the Minister, shall say:

With this ring I thee wed: in the name of the Father, and of the Son, and of the Holy Ghost. Amen.

[And, before delivering the ring to the man, the Minister may say as followeth:

Bless, O Lord, this ring, that he who gives it and she who wears it may abide in Thy peace, and continue in Thy favor, unto their life's end; through Jesus

Christ our Lord. Amen.]

The same procedure is followed if the woman is also giving a ring to the man.

Prayers

Then the Minister shall say,

Let us pray.

Then shall the Minister and the people, still standing, say the Lord's Prayer:

Our Father, who art in heaven, hallowed be Thy name. Thy kingdom come. Thy will be done, on earth as it is in heaven. Give us this day our daily bread. And forgive us our debts, as we forgive our debtors. And lead us not into temptation, but deliver us from evil. For Thine is the kingdom, and the power, and the glory, for ever and ever. Amen.

Then shall the Minister add:

O eternal God, Creator and Preserver of all mankind, Giver of all spiritual grace, the Author of everlasting life: send Thy blessing upon these Thy servants, this man and this woman, whom we bless in Thy name; that they, living faithfully together, may surely perform and keep the vow and covenant betwixt them made (whereof this ring [or these rings] given and received is a token and pledge), and may ever remain in perfect love and peace together, and live according to Thy laws; through Jesus Christ our Lord. Amen.

The Minister may add one of the following:

O Almighty God, Creator of mankind, who only art the wellspring of life: bestow upon these Thy servants, if it be Thy will, the gift and heritage of children; and grant that they may see their children brought up in Thy faith and fear, to the honor and glory of Thy name; through Jesus Christ our Lord. Amen.

O God, who hast so consecrated the state of matrimony that in it is represented the spiritual marriage and unity betwixt Christ and his church: look mercifully upon these Thy servants, that they may love, honor, and cherish each other, and so live together in faithfulness and patience, in wisdom and true godliness, that their home may be a haven of blessing and of peace; through the same Jesus Christ our Lord, who liveth and reigneth with Thee and the Holy Spirit ever, one God, world without end. Amen.

Declaration

Then shall the Minister join their right hands together, and say:

Those whom God hath joined together let no one put asunder.

Then shall the Minister speak unto the company:

Forasmuch as _____ and _____ have consented together in holy wedlock, and have witnessed the same before God and this company, and thereto have given and pledged their troth, each to the other, and have declared the same by giving and receiving a ring [or rings], and by joining hands, I pronounce that they are husband and wife, in the name of the Father, and of the Son, and of the Holy Spirit. Amen.

Benediction

The husband and wife kneeling, the Minister shall add this blessing:

God the Father, God the Son, God the Holy Spirit, bless, preserve and keep you; the Lord mercifully with his favor look upon you and fill you with all spiritual benediction and grace, that ye may so live together in this life, that in the world to come ye may have life everlasting. Amen.

Alternate Marriage Service #1[1]

The Christian marriage service should take place within the service for the Lord's day. At the time of the Offertory and after the gifts have been presented, a hymn is sung and the bride and groom and their company shall come from the congregation and take their places before the Table. If the marriage service is at another time, it ought to be in the setting of worship with suitable hymns, prayers, and Scripture readings.

The minister says:

Dear friends, _____ and _____ have come to offer themselves to God and each other in the holy bond of marriage.

God has established marriage for our welfare and enjoyment. Marriage makes sacred the union between man and woman and offers to each the opportunity to grow together in more complete manhood and womanhood.

Our Lord has declared that a man shall leave his parents and shall unite with his wife. He has commanded through his apostles that husbands and wives love and cherish each other throughout their lives and that they shall give each other strength and compassionate understanding and together share their joys and pains. The Creator offers to them the privilege and responsibility of parenthood and enjoins them that they support each other in this sacred opportunity with all affection and concern that their children might see in their marriage bond the love which comes from God and which offers hope to all.

These two who have heretofore traveled separate ways come now to be made one. If any here gathered can show any just cause why they may not lawfully be joined together in marriage, declare it now, or else forever hold your peace.

The minister addresses the two persons and says:

If either of you know any reason why you should not be joined in marriage, you must now confess it.

If no impediment appears, the minister says:

Let us pray:

Father of love, who hast brought these two together to be made one in holy marriage, all thy servants here assembled now pray thee to bless them with every good and perfect blessing. May their love never cease to grow in character and fullness; may they have the strength to share each other's joys and sorrows, continually bearing one another's burdens. May their temptations be few and may they always be ready to forgive each other, even as thou through Christ dost forgive them. We ask in the name of Jesus Christ, who has taught us to pray: Our Father . . .

Then the minister says to the man:

_____, will you have this woman to be your wedded wife, to live together in the holy estate of marriage? Will you love her, comfort her, honor and keep her, in sickness and in health; and forsaking all others keep you only to her, so long as you both shall live?

The man answers:

I will.

Then the minister says to the woman:

_____, will you have this man to be your wedded husband, to live together in the holy estate of marriage? Will you love him, comfort him, honor and keep him, in sickness and in health; and forsaking all others keep you only to him so long as you both shall live?

The woman answers:

I will.

Then the minister may say:

Who gives this woman to be married to this man?

The woman's father says:

Her mother and I do.

The minister then joins the right hands of the man and the woman. The man, instructed by the minister, says to the woman:

I, _____, take you, _____, to be my wife. I promise before God and these friends to be your loving and faithful husband, to share with you in plenty and in want, in joy and in sorrow, in sickness and in health, and to join with you so that together we may serve God and others, as long as we both shall live. God be my help.

While the hands are still joined, the woman, instructed by the minister, says to the man:

I, _____, take you, _____, to be my husband. I promise before God and these friends to be your loving and faithful wife, to share with you in plenty and in want, in joy and in sorrow, in sickness and in health, and to join with you so that together we may serve God and others, as long as we both shall live. God be my help.

They loose their hands and the minister asks for the ring(s) with these words:

What token have you to symbolize your pledge of the faithful fulfillment of your marriage vows?

Then the minister is given the ring(s) and says:

This ring (these rings) is (are) the outward and visible sign of the inward and spiritual bond which unites this man and woman in endless love.

The minister gives the ring to the man who places it upon the fourth finger of the woman's left hand. In the same way the woman may give a ring to the man. Then the man (followed by the woman, if there are two rings) repeats after the minister:

I give this ring to you as a token of the covenant made between us this day and as a pledge of our mutual love: in the name of the Father, and of the Son, and of the Holy Spirit. Amen.

Then the minister says to the congregation:

Since _____ and _____ have consented to join together in marriage, and have witnessed the same before God and this company, and have pledged their mutual love to each other, and have declared the same by the giving and receiving of a ring (rings), and by joining hands, I declare that they are husband and wife, in the name of the Father, and of the Son, and of the Holy Spirit. Amen.

The God of all love has joined you as husband and wife. Go now in peace, trusting that the love which you now know will forever make you one.

The couple may then kneel, as the minister says:

Let us pray:

Father of love and mercy, show thy compassion on this couple who have come before thee in the presence of their friends to pledge themselves to live together in the holy estate of marriage. Grant them the strength and patience, the affection and under-standing, the courage and love to abide together in peace and mutual growth according to thy will for them both; through Jesus Christ our Lord. Amen.

The minister may add this blessing:

The Lord bless you and keep you: The Lord make his face to shine upon you, and be gracious to you: The Lord lift up his countenance upon you, and give you peace. Amen.

Alternate Marriage Service #2 [2]

The parties standing before the minister, the man at the woman's right hand, and after prayer, or such other exercises as may be had, the minister shall say:

If it be your intention to take each other as husband and wife, you will manifest it by uniting your right hands.

This being done, he shall say to the man,

You now take this woman, whose hand you hold, to be your lawful wedded wife. Do you solemnly promise, before God and these witnesses, that you will love, honor, and cherish her; and that, forsaking all others for her alone, you will faithfully perform to her all the duties which a husband owes to a wife, so long as you both shall live?

He answers, I do. *Then to the woman,*

You now take this man, whose hand you hold, to be your lawful wedded husband. Do you solemnly promise, before God and these witnesses, that you will love, honor, and cherish him; and that, forsaking all others for him alone, you will faithfully perform to him all the duties which a wife owes to a husband, so long as you both shall live?

She answers, I do. *Then, if a ring be used, the minister shall take it from the man, and say to him,*

And this ring you give to her whom you have now taken as your lawful wife, in token of the affection with which you will cherish her, and the fidelity with which you will perform the sacred vows you have now made?

He answers, I do. *Then to her,*

And this ring you accept from him whom you have now taken as your lawful husband, and will wear as a sign and evidence of your affection for him, and the fidelity with which you will perform the sacred vows you have now made?

She answers, I do. *He then returns the ring to the man, directing him to place it on the hand of the woman. [This part of the service may be repeated if a second ring is used.] After which, he says:*

Let this be the seal of your plighted faith, and of

your mutual affection and fidelity; a memorial of this sacred service, and of the holy bonds of marriage, by which you are bound henceforth till death shall separate you.

As you have thus solemnly agreed before God and these witnesses, I pronounce you lawfully married husband and wife. May Divine favor crown this union and your future lives, with all temporal and spiritual blessings in Christ Jesus our Saviour, and bring you to the life everlasting. Amen.

Alternate Marriage Service #3 [3]

The parties standing before the minister, he shall say:

Marriage is a joyous occasion. It is connected in our thoughts with the magic charm of home, and with all that is pleasant and attractive in the tenderest and most sacred relations of life. When celebrated in Cana of Galilee, it was sanctioned and cheered by the presence of the Lord himself; and is declared by an inspired Apostle to be honorable in all.

And now, if you _____ and _____ have at present appeared for the purpose of being joined in legal wedlock, you will please to signify this intention, by uniting your right hands.

The minister shall then say to the man:

Do you take the woman whom you now hold by the hand, to be your lawful and wedded wife?

Answer, I do; *or, assent.*

Do you promise to love and cherish her, in sickness and in health, for richer or for poorer, for better or for worse, and forsaking all others keep thee only unto her, so long as you both shall live?

Answer, I do; *or assent. Then to the woman:*

Do you take the man who now stands by your side and who holds you by the hand, to be your lawful and wedded husband?

Answer, I do; *or assent.*

Do you promise, to love and cherish him, in sickness and in health, for richer or for poorer, for better or for worse, and forsaking all others, keep thee only unto him, so long as you both shall live?

Answer, I do; *or assent.*

You mutually promise in the presence of God, and of these witnesses, that you will at all times and in all circumstances, conduct yourselves toward one another as becometh Husband and Wife?

Both answer, I do; *or assent.*

That you will love, cherish, and adhere to one

another, until separated by death?

Both answer, I do; *or assent. If a ring is used, the minister will say to the Bridegroom:*

You will please place this ring on the hand of your affianced Bride . . . and reunite your hands.

If a second ring is to be given, a similar instruction will be given to the Bride. He shall continue:

Having taken these pledges of your affection and vows of fidelity, I do therefore, by authority of the laws of this State, sanctioned by divine authority, pronounce you _____ and _____, lawfully married, Husband and Wife; in the name of the Father, and of the Son, and of the Holy Spirit. Amen.

What, therefore, God hath joined together, let no one put asunder.

Prayer

---

1. From John E. Skoglund, *A Manual of Worship* (Valley Forge: Judson Press, 1968).
2. Contributed for this book by a friend of Dr. Hiscox.
3. Furnished by the Reverend Rollin H. Neal, D.D., of Boston, being the one used by him during his long ministry.

IV

The Funeral Service

IV

The Funeral Service

Each funeral service should be adapted to the particular situation of the person who has died. The service that follows conveys the elements of the Christian message and can be the basis for almost any occasion of last rites. For additional Scripture selections that you may wish to add or substitute, see the pages of "Selections from the Sacred Scriptures" elsewhere in this book, especially "Faith and Trust in God" (page 68), "Good Works" (page 93), "Children and Youth" (page 131), "Readings for the Sick and Shut-In" (page 137), "Death and Eternal Life" (page 141), "Grief" (page 145), "Comfort" (page 147), and "The Resurrection of Christ" (page 157).

Suggested texts for funeral sermons, as well as hymns for congregational use in a church funeral, are printed following the basic funeral service. It is suggested that funeral sermons be brief and to the point.

In preparing for funerals, you may also find it

helpful to review the section on "Funerals," which begins on page 39.

A Traditional Funeral Service

Introductory Scripture

Standing at the head of the casket after some introductory organ music, the pastor calls the mourners together with Scripture selections that provide comfort and that present the messages of God's loving care and Christ's call to salvation.

Jesus said, I am the resurrection and the life: he that believeth in me, though he were dead, yet shall he live: and whosoever liveth and believeth in me shall never die. *(John 11:25-26)*

I know that my redeemer liveth, and that he shall stand at the latter day upon the earth: and I shall see God: whom I shall see for myself, and mine eyes shall behold, and not another. *(Job 19:25-27)*

We brought nothing into this world, and it is certain we can carry nothing out. The Lord gave, and the Lord hath taken away; blessed be the name of the Lord. *(1 Timothy 6:7; Job 1:21)*

Eulogy

A eulogy may be spoken by the minister or a family member or some close friend or associate. In some situations there may be more than one speaker.

Scripture

In times of grief, we may find comfort in the Psalms. These selections are taken from the 39th and 90th Psalms:

Hear my prayer, O Lord, and give ear unto my cry; hold not thy peace at my tears: for I am a stranger with thee, and a sojourner, as all my fathers were. O spare me, that I may recover strength, before I go hence, and be no more. . . . Lord, thou hast been our dwelling place in all generations. Before the mountains were brought forth, or ever thou hadst formed the earth and the world, even from everlasting to everlasting, thou art God. For a thousand years in thy sight are but as yesterday when it is past, and as a watch in the night. They are as a sleep: In the morning they are like grass which groweth up; in the evening it is cut down, and withereth. So teach us to number our days, that we may apply our hearts unto wisdom.

We all find comfort in Psalm 23:

The Lord is my shepherd; I shall not want. He maketh me to lie down in green pastures: he leadeth me beside the still waters. He restoreth my soul: he leadeth me in the paths of righteousness for his name's sake. Yea, though I walk through the valley of the shadow of death, I will fear no evil: for thou art with me; thy rod and thy staff they comfort me. Thou preparest a table before me in the presence of mine enemies: thou anointest my head with oil; my cup runneth over. Surely goodness and mercy shall follow me all the days of my life: and I will dwell in the house of the Lord for ever.

We turn to the New Testament as we seek to understand Christ's offer of eternal life to those who respond to his bidding:

Let not your heart be troubled: ye believe in God, believe also in me. In my Father's house are many mansions: if it were not so, I would have told you. I go to prepare a place for you. And if I go and prepare a place for you, I will come again, and receive you unto myself; that where I am, there ye may be also. And whither I go ye know, and the way ye know. Thomas saith unto him, Lord, we know not whither thou goest; and how can we know the way? Jesus saith unto him, I am the way, the truth, and the life; no man cometh unto the Father, but by me. *(John 14:1-6)*

Now is Christ risen from the dead, and become the firstfruits of them that slept. For since by man came death, by man came also the resurrection of the dead. For as in Adam all die, even so in Christ shall all be made alive.

. . . But some men will say, How are the dead raised up? and with what body do they come? . . . All flesh is not the same flesh; but there is one kind of flesh of men, another flesh of beasts, another of fishes, and another of birds. There are also celestial bodies, and bodies terrestrial; but the glory of the celestial is one, and the glory of the terrestrial is another . . . .

So also is the resurrection of the dead. It is sown in corruption, it is raised in incorruption: it is sown in dishonor; it is raised in glory: it is sown a natural body; it is raised a spiritual body. There is a natural body, and there is a spiritual body. And so it is written, the first man Adam was made a living soul; the last Adam was made a quickening spirit . . . . The first man is of the earth, earthy: the second man is the Lord from heaven. As is the earthy, such are they also that are earthy: and as is the heavenly, such are they also that are heavenly. And as we have borne the image of the earthy, we shall also bear the image of the heavenly.

Now this I say, brethren, that flesh and blood cannot inherit the kingdom of God; neither doth corruption inherit incorruption. Behold, I show you a mystery: we shall not all sleep, but we shall all be changed, in a moment, in the twinkling of an eye, at the last trump: for the trumpet shall sound, and the dead shall be raised incorruptible, and we shall be changed. For this corruptible must put on incorruption, and this mortal must put on immortality.

So when this corruptible shall have put on incorruption, and this mortal shall have put on immortality; then shall be brought to pass the saying that is written, Death is swallowed up in victory. O death, where is thy sting? O grave, where is thy victory? The sting of death is sin; and the strength of sin is the law. But thanks be to God, which giveth us the victory through our Lord Jesus Christ. Therefore, my beloved brethren, be ye steadfast, unmovable, always abounding in the work of the Lord, forasmuch as ye know that your labor is not in vain in the Lord. *(Selected verses from 1 Corinthians 15)*

Funeral Sermon

A funeral sermon is optional. For suggested texts see pages 192-194.

Prayer

Dear Lord of us all, we give thee thanks for the life of the one who has been taken from us, for what he (she) has meant to the loving family and friends. (A few personal words may be inserted here.) We give thanks for the love of God and for the salvation that is freely offered to us by Jesus Christ. Bless us all, we pray in the name of the one who gave this prayer to his disciples: Our Father who art in heaven, hallowed be thy name. Thy kingdom come. Thy will be done on earth, as it is in heaven. Give us this day our daily bread. And forgive us our debts, as we forgive our debtors. And lead us not into temptation, but deliver us from evil: For thine is the kingdom and the power and the glory, forever. Amen.

Benediction

The grace of our Lord Jesus Christ, and the love of God, and the fellowship of the Holy Spirit be with us all evermore. Amen.

Service of Committal

Unless the burial is at a distant location, it is customary for the officiating minister to accompany the casket to the gravesite. Whenever the casket is carried, the minister precedes it. In the funeral procession, the minister may ride with the funeral director or drive his or her own car immediately behind the hearse. At the grave, a brief service of committal is appropriate:

Forasmuch as it hath pleased Almighty God, in his wise providence, to take out of this world unto himself the soul of our deceased brother (or sister, or friend), we therefore commit his (or her) body to the ground, earth to earth, ashes to ashes, dust to dust.

I heard a voice from heaven, saying unto me, Write, Blessed are the dead which die in the Lord from henceforth, saith the Spirit, that they may rest from their labors; and their works do follow them. *(Revelation 14:13)*

Benediction: Grace be unto you, and peace, from God our Father, and from the Lord Jesus Christ. Amen.

Suggested Texts for Funeral Sermons

Blessed is the man that walketh not in the counsel of the ungodly, nor standeth in the way of sinners, nor sitteth in the seat of the scornful. But his delight is in the law of the Lord; and in his law doth he meditate day and night. *(Psalm 1:1-2)*

Yea, though I walk through the valley of the shadow of death, I will fear no evil: for thou art with me; thy rod and thy staff they comfort me. *(Psalm 23:4)*

God is our refuge and strength, a very present help in trouble. *(Psalm 46:1)*

Let, I pray thee, thy merciful kindness be for my comfort, according to thy word unto thy servant. *(Psalm 119:76)*

Who can find a virtuous woman? for her price is far above rubies. . . . Give her of the fruit of her hands;

and let her own works praise her in the gates. *(Proverbs 31:10,31)*

Jesus said, Suffer little children, and forbid them not, to come unto me: for of such is the kingdom of heaven. *(Matthew 19:14)*

Come, ye blessed of my Father, inherit the kingdom prepared for you from the foundation of the world. *(Matthew 25:34)*

And Jesus took them up in his arms, put his hands upon them, and blessed them. *(Mark 10:16)*

And all wept, and bewailed her: but Jesus said, Weep not; she is not dead, but sleepeth. *(Luke 8:52)*

Jesus said: I am the resurrection, and the life: he that believeth in me, though he were dead, yet shall he live: and whosoever liveth and believeth in me shall never die. *(John 11:25-26)*

Jesus said: In my Father's house are many mansions: if it were not so, I would have told you. I go to prepare a place for you. *(John 14:2)*

Eye hath not seen, nor ear heard, neither have entered into the heart of man, the things which God hath prepared for them that love him. But God hath revealed them to us by his Spirit. *(1 Corinthians 2:9-10)*

For we know that if our earthly house of this

tabernacle were dissolved, we have a building of God, a house not made with hands, eternal in the heavens. *(2 Corinthians 5:1)*

Blessed are the dead which die in the Lord from henceforth: Yea, saith the Spirit, that they may rest from their labors; and their works do follow them. *(Revelation 14:13)*

And God shall wipe away all tears from their eyes; and there shall be no more death, neither sorrow, nor crying, neither shall there be any more pain: for the former things are passed away. *(Revelation 21:4)*

Suggested Hymns for Congregational Use at Funerals

Abide with Me
Amazing Grace
A Mighty Fortress Is Our God
Because He Lives
Be Still, My Soul
Be Thou My Vision
Beyond the Sunset
Breathe On Me, Breath of God
Come unto Me, Ye Weary
Come, Ye Disconsolate
For All the Saints Who from Their Labors Rest
From Every Stormy Wind That Blows

God Will Take Care of You
Good Night and Good Morning
Great Is Thy Faithfulness
Guide Me, O Thou Great Jehovah
He Leadeth Me! O Blessed Thought!
How Firm a Foundation
How Great Thou Art
I Know that My Redeemer Liveth
Immortal Love, Forever Full
In the Hour of Trial
It Is Well with My Soul
Jesus Is All the World to Me
Jesus, Savior, Pilot Me
Joyful, Joyful We Adore Thee
Lead, Kindly Light
Leaning on the Everlasting Arms
Love Divine, All Loves Excelling
Majestic Sweetness Sits Enthroned
My Faith Looks Up to Thee
My Jesus, As Thou Wilt
Near to the Heart of God
O God, Our Help in Ages Past
O Love That Wilt Not Let Me Go
O That Will Be Glory
Precious Lord, Take My Hand
Rock of Ages, Cleft for Me
Some Bright Morning

Sunrise Tomorrow
The King of Love My Shepherd Is
The Old Rugged Cross
There's a Land that Is Fairer than Day
Thine Is the Glory
We Cannot Think of Them as Dead
We'll Understand It Better By and By
We're Marching to Zion
What a Friend We Have in Jesus
When Morning Dawns
When the Roll Is Called Up Yonder
When We All Get to Heaven

V

Parliamentary Considerations for Churches

V

Parliamentary Considerations for Churches

Constitution and Bylaws. The church should have a constitution giving such basic information as its name, purpose, qualifications for membership, affiliations, and the procedures for dissolution. Amendment of the constitution should be rather difficult, requiring a specific number of weeks' advance notice, and a favorable vote of two-thirds or three-fourths of those present.

The bylaws provide operating rules such as the election, responsibilities, and procedure for termination of the pastor; the terms and responsibilities of church officers; the composition, terms, and duties of the church council, boards, and standing committees; also the calling of meetings; the submission of reports; the period of the fiscal year; and similar matters. Amendment of the bylaws should require

advance notice, but perhaps a shorter time than for
the constitution; also, a lower requirement of favorable votes to amend.

Meetings. Every church should have an annual
meeting for the election of officers, the receiving of
annual reports, and the transaction of any business
that members might wish to propose. The dating of
the annual meeting is specified in the bylaws. Many
churches will also have other stated meetings, quar-
terly or monthly, the times for which should also be
specified in the bylaws. In addition, special meetings
may be called to deal with specific matters. The
procedure for calling these should appear in the
bylaws. Usually it involves a request from the church
council or one of the boards, or the submission of a
petition by a required number of members.

Moderator. The moderator is the presiding officer at church meetings. In some churches this responsibility is assigned *ex officio* to the pastor, but there
are advantages to having a lay person elected as
moderator for at least two reasons: (1) It helps to
reduce the pastor's burden of duties, and (2) it provides for automatic leadership during an interim
when there is no pastor. The bylaws should indicate
who is the substitute in the event that the moderator
is unable to serve at a particular time. For example,
the chairperson of the diaconate may be first in

succession for this responsibility, and a second in line might also be designated.

Church Clerk. The church clerk is responsible for taking accurate minutes of all church meetings and customarily also of meetings of the church council. The church clerk also maintains the membership records of the church unless this duty has been assigned to the church office.

The Members. All regular members have equal rights and privileges in church meetings, an equal interest in the successful outcome of the deliberations, and an equal responsibility to maintain an orderly and productive meeting. If the church has some form of associate membership, the constitution may place certain limits on their participation.

Order of Business. For an annual meeting or other stated meeting, it is helpful if the moderator prepares an order of business or agenda and distributes copies to those present. It should provide for opening devotions, reading and approval of the preceding meeting's minutes, committee reports, unfinished business (itemized), new business (listing any that is expected to be brought before the meeting), and adjournment. It is helpful if a few moments are taken at the beginning of the meeting to review the agenda and allow opportunity for deletions or additions. With respect to special meetings, their purpose is stated in the call for the meeting, and only the specified business can be considered.

Quorum. The bylaws should specify the number or percentage of members whose attendance is required to create a quorum. In setting this figure the church should choose a figure high enough to provide a reasonable representation but low enough that a quorum can usually be attained. At the beginning of a meeting the moderator should determine that a quorum is present and so announce it. Any member can require a count at any time by saying: "I suggest the absence of a quorum." If a quorum is not present, no official action can be taken, but those present can continue to discuss the issues.

Motions. Any proposed action is presented by a member through a motion, preferably given in writing to the moderator and church clerk for accuracy. The motion should ordinarily be seconded by another member, though it is considered to be automatically seconded if it is the product of a committee action.

Only one motion can properly come before a meeting at a time, but there are certain special motions which by common usage may interrupt one already under debate. These include motions to amend, to substitute, to refer to committee, to postpone, to lay on the table, to reconsider, to call up the previous question, and to adjourn.

Amendments. Motions can be amended by omitting, adding, or substituting words or sentences. An amendment may itself be amended, but no amending is acceptable beyond this point. When there is an amendment on the floor, discussion is on this (not on the original motion), which must be acted upon before the original motion. If the amendment passes, the meeting can then discuss and vote on the original motion as amended. If not, the discussion reverts to the original motion as it was before the amendment was proposed. The procedure is similar when there is an amendment to the amendment: Act first on the amendment to the amendment, then on the amendment as amended (if it is), and finally on the main motion as amended (if it is). Always remember that the approval or defeat of a proposed amendment does not in itself constitute action on the main motion. Another vote is required.

Although it is not strictly approved by parliamentary authorities, there is a common practice that has the merit of simplification, which allows the maker of a motion to amend it with the consent of the seconder.

Debate on motions. Any member desiring to speak should rise in place and address the moderator, confining all remarks to the motion under discussion. The moderator will attempt to recognize persons with various points of view to allow fair debate, making a special point of recognizing persons who have not spoken, in preference to those who have. If someone interrupts by calling for the question, the moderator should ask for a show of hands as to whether the group is ready to vote. When the moderator believes discussion is dying down, it is appropriate to ask "Are you ready for the question?" and put the matter to a vote unless it is clear that others need to be heard.

Voting. Most motions can be decided by a simple call for a spoken "Aye" or "No." If there is doubt, a standing vote should be called for, with designated tellers to count those standing. It is also possible to have secret written ballots, and this is a good idea if the issue is one that might cause some members to be embarrassed by their votes. In case of written ballots, they should be counted in another room by tellers, and the results of the tally reported to the meeting. In any case, the moderator announces the result of the vote—that the motion is passed or lost.

Appeals. Although the moderator's rulings are usually accepted without objection, any member has the right to appeal a decision. In that case the moderator puts the question, "Shall the decision of the chair be sustained?" and the members decide by majority vote whether to accept the ruling or not.

Special motions. A motion for the previous question, duly seconded, cannot be debated, and if passed cuts off all further discussion of the main motion, forcing a vote.

A motion to lay on the table, duly seconded, is not debatable. This is intended to set aside a main motion for later discussion, which can be initiated in due time by a motion to take from the table. The motion to lay on the table is sometimes used improperly to kill a motion that is under consideration.

A motion to postpone to a specific time, duly seconded, can if passed require that the main motion will be further considered at that time. If the motion is to postpone indefinitely, it effectively kills the main motion.

A motion to reconsider, duly seconded, is debatable if the original motion was debatable, otherwise not. If passed, it recalls an earlier motion for further consideration. It can be made only by a person who voted on the prevailing side.

A motion to refer to a committee, duly seconded, is debatable, and is used when the members believe the issue needs further study by a smaller group. It is assumed that the committee will report back at a later meeting and thus bring the issue to the floor again.

A motion to adjourn, duly seconded, is always in

order except while someone is speaking or a vote is being taken. It is not debatable and takes precedence over any other motion.

VI

Ecclesiastical Forms and Blanks

VI

Ecclesiastical Forms and Blanks

Ecclesiastical forms and blanks have no fixed or necessary wording. They will vary according to the customs of the churches and the taste of those who prepare them. The following present substantially the forms in common use:

Letter of Dismission

The _____ Church of _____
To the _____ Church of _____

Dear Friends:
This is to certify, that _____ is a member of this church in good and regular standing, and at _____ own request is hereby dismissed from us for the purpose of uniting with you. When _____ shall have so united, _____ connection with us will cease. May the blessing of

God rest on _____ and you.
Done by order of the Church.

Date_____
_____, *Clerk*

This letter is valid for six months from stated date.

Letter of Notification

Date _____
To the _____ Church.

Dear Friends:
This certifies that _____ was received by
letter from you, to membership in the _____
Church, *Date* _____.

_____, *Clerk*

License to Preach

This certifies that _____ is a member of the
_____ Church, in good and regular standing, and is held by us in high esteem, and is worthy
of this license to preach the gospel. We believe this
person to have been called of God to the work of the
gospel ministry, and we do hereby give our entire and
cordial approval in the improvement of spiritual

gifts, by preaching the gospel, as Providence may afford opportunity. And we pray the great Head of the Church to bestow all needful grace, and crown this ministry with abundant success.

Done by order of the church, this day, _____(month), _____(day), _____(year).

_____, *Pastor*

_____, *Clerk*

Certificate of Ordination

This certifies that _____ was publicly set apart to the work of the gospel ministry, with prayer and the laying on of hands, by the authority of the _____ Church, and according to the usages of our denomination, at _____,

_____,

_____(month), ____(day), ____(year).

That _____ churches were represented in the council, by _____ ministers, and _____ laypersons; and that after a full, fair, and deliberate examination, being satisfied on all points, the council did unanimously recommend the candidate's ordination.

That _____ did accordingly receive the full, entire, and hearty approval of the council upon the work of the ministry, preaching the Word, adminis-

tering the ordinances, and performing all those duties, and enjoying all those privileges, to which a
minister of Christ is called and entitled.

_____, *Moderator*
_____, *Clerk*
Date _____

*Note: Ordination certificates may be purchased from
some religious book and supply stores.*

Call for an Ordaining Council

State _____, *Date* _____
To the _____ Church of _____

Dear Friends:
You are requested to send your pastor and two other
members to sit in council with us, (*date*)
_____, at (*time*) _____, to consider
the propriety of setting apart to the work of the gospel
ministry, our member _____.
The council will meet in _____.
The following churches are invited _____.
By order of the Church,

_____, *Clerk*

Call for a Recognizing Council

State _____, *Date* _____

To the _____ Church in _____

Dear Friends:

In behalf of a company of believers in Christ, you are requested to send your pastor and two other members to meet in council at _____, *(date)* _____, at *(time)* _____, to consider the propriety of recognizing said company of believers as a regular and independent church.

The council will meet in _____.

The following churches are invited _____.

By order of the Church,

_____, *Clerk*

ISBN 0-8170-0167-0

9 780817 001674